Financial Supervision in a Comparative Perspective

Margherita Poto

Financial Supervision in a Comparative Perspective

intersentia

METRO

Ius Commune Europaeum

Margherita Poto

Financial Supervision in a Comparative Perspective

ISBN 978-94-000-0048-3
D/2010/7849/51
NUR 828

FOREWORD AND ACKNOWLEDGMENTS

Supervision in financial markets has followed different paths in the European system. One of the approaches useful to track them is the comparative analysis. The key point of the present work has focused on the necessity to find out both a constitutive model and a functional model of the authorities in charge of the financial supervision. In this sense, the German and the Anglo-American systems have been deeply scrutinized.

Both the models have been studied using a bipartite parameter: firstly, a comparative study on the powers and missions of the financial supervisory authorities; secondly an analysis of the responsibilities and liabilities, through the lenses of the legislative sources and the decisions of the Courts. The European case law has been the seismograph to test the overall situation.

The descriptive part of the work has been then evaluated from a critical perspective, involving historical, sociological and economical remarks, which formed the first two chapters of the book.

The second reading of the work can be considered as a roundtable for discussions, about the feasibility of a model of supervision through independent authorities. In this occasion, some perplexities regarding the efficiency of such a choice have been arisen.

This book aims to provide a new perspective on the role of the financial supervisory authorities, with some critical hints regarding the effectiveness of their activities.

* *
*

The present work is a reviewed and updated version of my Doctoral studies conducted in Italy and in Germany in 2003/2006. The English translation has been lovely cured by Elisabeth Poore and John B. Wilson.

Firstly, I thank them, and the little one who patiently waited for her father to finish his job.

Secondly, I thank Ania Salinas and Oswald Jansen, whose friendship and support made this publication possible.

Finally, I thank Elsa Bianchi, the most perseverant, generous and passionate worker I have ever met.

Questo libro è per te, nonna, con immenso amore.

Wageningen, 8 February 2010

CONTENTS

Chapter 1

CHAPTER 1. THE THEORETICAL SUBSTRATUM

1. Towards the decline of national sovereignty

The consolidation of the European system is an aim that generations of scholars and statesmen have long sought, since 18 April 1951, when the treaty that established the European Coal and Steel Community (ECSC), now defunct, was signed in Paris. This was followed by the establishment of the European Economic Community (EEC) and European Atomic Energy Community on 25 March 1957 with the Treaty of Rome.[1]

But this is well-known.

The intention of this introduction is to not linger excessively on the main stages which have marked the long path leading to the formation of a new kind of legal order, but rather, to explore the historical and philosophical context from where this system gathered inspiration and which enabled its development.

In other words, we need to provide an introduction to this topic of the independent authorities assigned to the oversight of financial markets by outlining both the historic and economic background, the warp and the weft of the European system, where these authorities have emerged and now operate.

The two aspects will be analyzed with particular attention given to the philosophical thinking which has followed their development in terms of theory, with attention to key notions as regards finance, and the stages achieved at the community level of supervision as regards economics.

In addition a comparison will be made between the German and British legal models, with the purpose of providing some examples of independent authorities operating in

1 The EEC Treaty's original full name was the Treaty establishing the European Economic Community, but in 1993 the Treaty of Maastricht changed the name of the EEC treaty to reflect the change of the EEC in becoming the European. Hence the treaty became the Treaty establishing the European Community (TEC). If the Treaty of Lisbon comes into force as planned, a further change in the nature of the Community would lead to the EEC treaty being amended and renamed as the Treaty on the Functioning of the European Union (TFEU) On this topic see in literature: L. Daniele, *Diritto del mercato unico europeo. Cittadinanza – Libertà di circolazione – Concorrenza – Aiuti di Stato*, Milano, 2006; G. Tesauro, *Diritto comunitario*, III ed., Padova, 2003. J. Steiner, L. Woods, C. Twigg-Flesner, *EU Law*, 9th edition, Oxford University Press, Oxford, 2006.

the financial sector in order to determine characteristics, powers, functions and responsibilities.

It is now necessary to look back to 1951 when the need arose to create a specialized administrative agency with international and supranational traits.

The idea of setting up a third party organism in relation to the single member states was in some ways revolutionary within the ideological and political context in which it was conceived, imbued with the persuasive force of Weber's distinction between the public and private domain, and between economic and public rationality; this distinction, which will be discussed below, marked the transition from the 19th to the 20th century until its progressive erosion after the second world war.[2]

It was a sensationally powerful idea: to create institutions separate from member states, with the goal of regulating economic relations, facilitating trade, and increasing flexibility during negotiations.

This idea has succeeded in inserting itself like a wedge between the apparently unassailable opposition between public and private, the "two extremes upheld by different principles and rules", the distinction which Weber made himself a spokesman for.

In contemporary Italian legal literature, Cassese demonstrated that fundamentally, if compared within today's European framework, these two forms of rationality are not so radically different. He did this by analyzing the supervision of certain specific sectors (paying particular attention to telecommunications) in which independent authorities have been operating for some time.[3]

This conclusion led him to admit the possibility of interaction between various public authorities, and between public authorities and private actors. Therefore it can be said that public rationality in a sense uses the market's categories and rules of engagement.

It is now necessary to analyze these concepts to see how they gradually developed; there is a particular need to comprehend the reasons why the notion of national sovereignty has undergone revision, and, attacked on a number of sides, seems today to be changing.

"Suddenly, as blow knocks shield, the force of the wind cuts in", we read in a poem by D'Annunzio, "The Wave", from his work "Halcyon". If sovereignty is a wave, the strength of the wind, of other waves, of other power centres, have surely cut into it.[4]

Metaphors aside, it is clear that a long hard effort is required to bring together of the concept of national sovereignty with the concept of integration between separate centres of power: the States, lords of the Treaties (*Herren der Verträge)* must come to terms with new entities, which they themselves have established, with specialized agencies, committees and independent authorities, endowed with specific functions, but all true to the common principle of fair cooperation.[5]

2 See S. Cassese, *La spazio giuridico globale*, Bari, 2003, 138. During the present work, I will mainly refer to M. Weber, *Wirtschaft und Gesellschaft*, Mohr/Siebeck, Tübingen, 1921, 1976.

3 S. Cassese, *Lo spazio giuridico globale cit.*, 138.

4 Translation of "L'Onda", by G. D'Annunzio: "A un tratto, come colpo dismaglia l'arme, la forza del vento l'intacca".

5 See the website: www.europa.eu/agencies/community_agencies/index.htm, consulted in May 2008. A. Dammann, *Die Bechwerdekammern der europäischen Agenturen*, in *Schriften zum Europa – und*

The considerations regarding this point made by G. Berti are fitting: "The history of the past two centuries, characterized by legal positivism, itself the outcome of secularisation, is full of problems related to the definition of society-State relations through the law. When states recognise themselves and isolate themselves in their domestic domain, as has been the case particularly in the last century, they want to elevate politics as society's guardian and they make use of their sovereignty and the system which accompanies it to influence the legitimacy of the sources of social, or non-state production. [...] The situation, thus summarised, is however rapidly changing. The market economy, ally of the quasi paroxysmal communication between human beings and peoples, is causing the myths and symbols of territorial states to gradually fall".[6]

Firstly, it seems therefore essential to comprehend the notions of sovereignty, of power and of citizens' obedience to a pre-established order.[7] Classical doctrine raises many interesting doubts: "In truth, so much has been said or written on the concept of sovereignty, but still today there are many more doubts than certainties. Is sovereignty a legal notion or a fact? And in this second case, is it a structural and political, and therefore meta-legal, fact? Is it a product of law, or rather its absolute source of power, even inaccessible and indivisible? Is there a limit, and if so what is it, to the exercise of sovereignty, particularly expressed in a democratic system by the representative body, that is by Parliament? Can one divide sovereignty and share it, without risking losing it?".[8]

To answer such questions it is necessary to analyze the concepts of sovereignty and power, as they emerge from the pages of *Wirtschaft und Gesellshaft*, in order to understand their gradual disintegration.

Thus a short analysis is necessary, prior to any reflection on the problems of regulation, of this work, *Wirtschaft und Gesellshaft*, that has been defined as the "Mammoth of the 20th century"[9], and meticulously studied by generations of jurists, one of the most important being Jurgen Habermas. This analysis will enable us to go on to discuss the modern debate on the crisis of the democratic model in Europe and any possibility of relaunching it.

Völkerrecht und zur Rechtvergleichung, Peter Lang, Europäischer Verlag des Wissenschaften, Frankfurt am Main, 2004.

6 G. Berti, *Diffusione della normatività e nuovo disordine delle fonti del diritto*, in G. Gitti (ed.), *L'autonomia privata e le autorità indipendenti. La metamorfosi del contratto*, Bologna, 2006, 28.

7 G. Rebuffa, *Max Weber e la scienza del diritto*, Torino, 1989, 13.

8 G. Tesauro, *Sovranità degli Stati e integrazione comunitaria*, in *Diritto dell'Unione Europea*, 2006, 235.

9 J.P. McCormick, *Max Weber and Jürgen Habermas: The Sociology and Philosophy of Law During Crises of the State*, in *Yale Journal of Law and Humanities*, 1997, 300: "the sociology of law elaborated in Weber's mammoth Economy and Society in many ways sets the agenda for Habermas' legal philosophy...I will argue here that in order fully to understand Habermas's theoretical efforts in Between facts and Norms one must take into account the legal-sociological framework that he inherits from Max Weber. [...] [F]or Weber's sociology of law played a crucial role in the historical drama that was the collapse of Germany's first effort at liberal and social democracy: the Weimar Republic. It is the ghost of this failure that has haunted virtually all of Habermas's theoretical endeavours, no less Between Facts and Norms – perhaps even especially therein because of the centrality of law to its framework".

2. Max Weber and the notion of sovereignty

Max Weber's writings are of great relevance to comprehension of modern capitalist societies.

His thinking, the product of careful survey of economic and legal history, make it possible to define the main characteristics, the origins and the destiny of these societies.

The origin of western capitalism is pinpointed by Weber in specific forms of European culture at the beginning of the modern age, and that is in forms of religious culture. This is the idea he develops in the essay *The Protestant Ethic and the Spirit of Capitalism*[10], which is then taken up again in *Wirtschaft und Gesellshaft*, whose publication was attended to by his pupils.

After examining the different levels of rationalisation attained by the leading world religions, Max Weber identifics a link between the Protestant faith and the foundations of capitalism. Capitalism, according to Weber, is an expression of the secularisation of society, and the Protestant ethic, amongst many other manifestations of religiosity, epitomises its authentic meaning, its "Spirit": "Kapitalismus" hat es auf dem Boden aller deiser Religiositäten gegeben. Eben sochen wie es [hin] in der oksidentalen Antike und im abendländischen Mittelalter auch gab. Aber keine Entwicklung, auch keine Ansätze einer solchen, zum modernen Kapitalismus und vor alle: keinen "kapitalistischen Geist" in dem Sinn, wie er dem asketischen Protestantismus eignete.

This connection is, according to Weber, summed up in the renowned phrase ascribed to Benjamin Franklin: "Time is money", intended as it were in a spiritual sense: "It is infinitely precious, because every lost hour is taken from work in the service of God. Without value, if not indeed indecent, is idle contemplation, at least when it occurs at the expense of professional labour".[11]

Protestantism indeed portrays a series of features which are thought to be beneficial to the capitalist spirit, such as a focus on the individual as regards faith, and the idea of profession as a calling, expressed by the German term *Beruf*.[12]

The observations of a great scholar of Protestantism, R.H. Bainton, are interesting in this regard: "What part did religion, and in particular Protestantism, have in all this growth? If capitalism must be defined in terms of loans, credit, accounting and banking activity, it must be said that this process is inextricable from the financial activities of the Catholic Church, which made ample use of the services offered by Italian and German banks, and especially of the big financiers such as the Welsers and the Fuggers. But if capitalism is instead considered as a view of life that is distinguished by incessant activity, then it is to Protestantism that not only a general affinity but also actual paternity are largely attributed".[13]

It is the inscrutability of divine judgement which makes the work dimension and methodic professionality so central: success at work can be perceived as a sign of God's

10 M. Weber, *The Protestant Ethic and the Spirit of the Capitalism*, firstly published in 1905. See the edition by *Penguin Books, 2002* translated by *Peter Baehr and Gordon C. Well.*

11 B. Franklin, *Advice to a Young Tradesman* (1748).

12 M. Weber, *The Protestant Ethic and the Spirit of the Capitalism cit.*, 59.

13 R. Bainton, *The Reformation of the Sixteenth Century*, Boston, The Beacon Press, 1952, 23.

benevolence. In this sense Weber speaks of *ascesis within the world*: "because Protestants adhere to the material world in the accomplishment of their *Beruf*, but at the same time are ascetic as regards the world because of their renunciation of all earthly delights and flight from all temptation".[14]

This point raises questions as to what could be the reason which drives humans to obey the law. If there exists an established rational order, a state authority that holds it, what is the reason which makes the community agree to it?

In answering this question, Max Weber applies the so-called "typological method", according to which analysis of social phenomena can and must be broken down into the study of individual behaviours, by means of analysis of the uniformity of such behaviours as regards the rules and dictates of authority.

According to Weber there is a close connection between the concept of obedience and the need to rationalise the world. It resides in the need to build around the principle "time is money" a grid of criteria on the basis of which this principle is applied, and to define the scope of its legitimacy. This principle must, fundamentally, be translated, systematised, in "rational criteria", in which all individuals may identify themselves. This is effectively expressed by Barbara Thériault: "Si les Puritans de l'éthique protestante s'accordent sur la phrase "Le temps, c'est de l'argent" – et, par ricochet, sur le principe de rentabilité – ils doivent cependant spécifier quand, comment, dans quelles circonstances et selon quels critères la maxime s'applique; bref, ils doivent définir son contexte de validité. Parce-qu'elles sont sujettes à de multiples interprétations, les maximes doivent être traduites, codifiées, en "critères de rationalité"[15].

The answer to the question concerned with the uniformity of individual behaviours towards the rules laid down by the holders of power lies in the activity that Weber calls "ethically rationalizing the world": by purifying oneself of every spiritual inhibition, individual action becomes economic action, endowed with high moral significance.[16]

The introduction to Economic History says: "What in the ultimate analysis has created capitalism is a permanent enterprise of a rational nature, rational accounting, rational technology, rational law, but not only. To these factors others needed to be added, in completion: the rational mentality, rationalisation of the conduct of everyday life, and

14 M. Weber, Geistige Arbeit als Beruf. Vorträge vor dem Freistudentischen Bund. Erster Vortrag. Prof. Max Weber (München) Wissenschaft als Beruf, München/Leipzig, Duncker und Humblot, 1919.

15 B. Thériault, *Ordres légitimes et légitimité des ordres chez Max Weber*, 179, in M. Coutou and G. Rocher (cur. by), *La légitimité de l'État et du droit. Autour de Max Weber*, L.G.D.J. et les Presses de l'Université Laval, Paris, 2006; V. M. Weber, *Soziologische Grundbegriffe cit.*, 62. See also M. Coutou, *Max Weber et les rationalités du droit*, L.G.D.J. et les Presses de l'Université Laval, Paris, 1997, which contains an analysis of the rational criteria: "1. L'action rationnelle en finalité (zweckrational), orientée d'après les fins, moyens et conséquences subsidiaires; [...] 2. l'action rationnelle en valeur (wertrational), fondée sur la croyance en valeur intrinsèque inconditionnelle [...] d'un comportement déterminé; 3. l'action affectuelle (affecktuel), fonction de l'émotion, du sentiment momentané; 4. l'action traditionnelle (traditional), laquelle repose sur l'observation quasi-mécanique de ce qui est coutumier".

16 M. Weber, *WG cit.*, 379 states: "Nur der asketische Protestantismus machte der Magie, der Außerweltlichkeit der Heilssuche und der Intellektualistischen kontemplativen 'Erleuchtung' als deren höchster Form wirklich den Garaus, nur er schuf die religiöse motive, gerade in der Bemühung im innerweltlichen 'Beruf' [...] das Heil zu suchen".

the rational economic ethos". With these words Weber summarises the meaning of his teachings. The Protestant ethic appears, in the end, as the decisive factor in the rise of capitalism: a factor which adds to all the others that had formed in the previous centuries.[17]

The idea of obedience is connected to the idea of power which, as has already been said, represents the heart of Weberian thinking. The word "power" must be interpreted as meaning the possibility for specific commands (or any command) to be followed by part of a given group of human beings, and not the possibility of exercising "power" (Macht) and "influence" (Einfluß) on other human beings: "'Herrschaft' soll, definitiongemäß, die Chance heißen, für spezifische (oder: für alle) Befehle bei einer angebbaren Gruppe von Menschen Gehorsam zu finden. Nicht also jede Art von Chance 'Macht' und 'Einfluß' im Einzefall auf den verschiedensten Motiven der Fügsamkeit".[18]

Among the factors which determine this liberation from the straitjacket of a traditional type of obedience is the market directed economy oriented towards the meeting of demand and the supply of goods and services. Historically the transition from an agrarian economy to a market economy was complex and not without obstacles. Weber examines this development from the viewpoint of a progressive "objectivisation" of relationships (not by chance he dedicates ample space to the notion of the "contract" as the ideal instrument to discipline relations among individuals) and of their related rationalisation: "Die Marktgemeindschaft als solche ist die unpersönlichste praktische Lebensbeziehung, in welche Menschen miteinander treten können".[19]

In short, the rationalisation of relations involves their "depersonalisation".

From the individual to the collective, from an individual's action to the rationalisation of conduct in a pattern, or better rather, in a network of rationally calculated behaviours.

I use the term "network", because it is precisely this notion that will constitute the means for transforming the public-private dichotomy – to which, however, Weber, *fils de son siècle*, remains inevitably anchored – to a system based on the parcelling out of powers.[20]

The market order is, therefore, not only a mere vessel for distributory relationships, but becomes a system for the organisation of social, economic and political relations, to which bonds and ties of a personal nature remain completely extraneous: "Der Markt ist in vollem Gegensatz zu allen anderen Vergemeinschaften, die immer persönliche brüderung und meist Blutverwandtsschaften voraussetzen, jeder Verbrüderung in der Wurzel fremd".[21]

The suggested conception of work as *Beruf*, as vocation, places the individual in a dimension in which he becomes "the absolute goal of himself", and, at the same time, the

17 *WG*, I, 122.

18 Ibidem.

19 M. Weber, *Wirtschaft und Gesellschaft*, 382.

20 C.P. Guarini, *Contributo allo studio della regolazione "indipendente" del mercato*, Bari, 2005, 13.

21 *WG*, 383. See *amplius* G. Rebuffa, *Nel crepuscolo della democrazia*, Bologna, 1992, 84 and K. Polanyi, *The Great Transformation*, 1944, New York, Holt, Rinehart & Winston Inc., 1944.

rational organisation of work is the road towards the establishment of a system based on companies. Rebuffa's comment on this point is: "Rationalization of economic relations, intended as the matching of means to ends, in the sense of maximum predictability of outcomes, implies an unprecedented extension of legal regimentation, and the penetration of rules into all aspects of public and private life".[22]

From the collective to the individual, whose actions respond to a rational logic, intertwining with those of other individuals, in an organized web of relations, regulated by the logic of the market.

It must be emphasised, for the purposes of this dissertation, that there is an intimate connection between the dynamics of the economy and the need to give these dynamics a legal form, through the law.

For Weber, economics and law are two complementary forces, whose relations are well defined. To quote *Economic History*: "Finally, it is necessary to emphasise again that the history of economics [...] does not coincide with the history of the whole of human civilisation, as the *materialistic vision of history* would like us to believe. Civilisation is not a result, but only a function of that; rather the history of economics constitutes only an underlying structure. However, without an understanding of it, fruitful investigation of any great area of civilisation is impossible".[23]

This statement requires further clarification concerning Weber's vision of relations between law and economics.

As commentators have pointed out, generally for Weber legal phenomena are not directly influenced by economic factors, since they depend on intra-legal relations and also on the political conditions (the example given concerns the power interests of an absolute sovereign against class privileges, particularly against a system of justice which is not under their control).

However, legal and economic relations may influence each other, if one observes them from a "reverse" perspective, as it were: if rational law is indeed independent from capitalistic development, it precedes it in a certain sense, and is a favourable precondition to it, since legal rationalisation provides an incentive to capitalism.

Therefore rational capitalism, a consequence of the combination of the work effort of single individuals, and liberated from the yoke of tradition and mere obedience to religious precepts, acquires the language of law, and attends to the selection and propagation of certain patterns. This does not mean that economic situations automatically

22 G. Rebuffa, *op. ult. cit.*, 88. See also F. Tessitore, *Storicismo*, 513, in P. Rossi (dir. by), *La Filosofia*, vol. IV, *Stili e modelli teorici del Novecento*, Torino, 1995: "Quest'è il disancantamento dal mondo, prodotto di una lunga storia, che parte dal mondo greco e arriva alla matura modernità".

23 See M. Weber, Economic History, *cit.*, 44; K. Löwith, *Max Weber und Karl Marx*, 1932; R. Roth, *Das historische Verhältnis der weberschen Soziologie zum Marxismus*, in *Kölner Zeitschrift für Sociologie und Sozialpsychologie*, XX, 1968, 429; W.J. Mommsen, *Max Weber als Kritiker der Marxismus*, in *Zeitschrift für Sociologie*, III, 1974, 256; F. Ferrarotti, *L'orfano di Bismarck: Max Weber e il suo tempo*, Roma, 1982, 82; A. Roversi, *Weber e Marx: le premesse storiche e concettuali di un confronto*, in *Quaderni di sociologia*, XXXIV, 2/3, 1985, 207.

generate new legal forms, but rather that they do not oppose the possibility [Chance] that a technical-legal invention, once created, will succeed in proliferating.[24]

This is where the metamorphosis of the notion of "power" begins: where in a pre-capitalist economy power was identified with subjects' obedience to a preconstituted order, with the development of capitalism, the depersonalisation of relationships and their consequent rationalisation, causes it to become a favourable condition for the spread of commerce.

"Macht bedeutet Chance" Weber repeats on more than one occasion. It is also true that, in and for itself, the concept of power, Macht, is sociologically amorphous: "Der Begriff 'Macht' ist soziologisch amorph".[25] It could mean obedience towards a sovereign will, justified by an ethical, religious feeling, but experiences a transformation when there is a change in the historical context in which it arises. Thus it adopts the form of a positive circumstance, when the context is cleansed of personalisation of relationships; when, that is, as we have already seen, a market economy develops, in a series of "economically oriented" behaviours ("Wirtschaftlift orientiert").[26]

But now let us return to the logical stages which, in the works of the German sociologist, mark the relations between economics and law. According to Weber, first and foremost rational law is independent of the development of capitalism. It may be considered by the same standards as an extra-economic condition which influences the development of entrepreneurial capitalism; but it is capitalism – market economics – that, making use of technical-legal patterns, provides for their selection and diffusion.

The relation between legal and economic systems can be sought in the distribution of effective power to regulate economic goods and services.[27]

The distribution of goods and services according to the logic of efficiency and rationalisation is an abstract guarantee of power; in other words, it ensures that players can put themselves in a favourable condition, thus contributing to the creation of formally rational law and the establishment of an organised system, in which rules replace privilege.

This, according to Weber, is the explanation of the relationship between law and economics, whose foundations, as we have seen, are based on the complementariness of the one to the other, without creating the dependency of the latter on the former. Law does not guarantee any economic interest considered in and for itself, but since an

24 M. Weber, *Soziologische Grundbegriffe*, 6. erneut durchgesehene Auflage, mit einer Einführung von Johannes Winckelmann, J.C.B. Mohr (Paul Siebeck), Tübingen, 1921, 1984, 47: "in der Chance, daß in einer (Sinnhaft) angebarren Art sozial gehandelt wird, einerlei zunächst: worauf diese Chance beruht". See also on the topic L.M. Friedman, *On Legalistic Reasoning. A Footnote to Weber*, in *Wisconsin Law Review*, 1966, 148.

25 M. Weber, *WG cit.*, 28.

26 M. Weber, *WG cit.*, 31.

27 M. Weber, *WG*, 181: "Danarch bestimmt sich auch die prinzipielle Beziehung zwischen Recht und Wirtschaft. [...] Die durch die Art des Interessenausgleichs jeweils einverständnismäßig entstandene Verteilung der faktischen Verfügungsgewalt über Güter und ökonomische Dienste und die Art, wie beide Kraft jener auf Einverständnis ruhenden faktischen Verfügungsgewalt dem gemeinten Sinn nach tatsächlich verwendet werden, nennen wir 'Wirtschaftsordnung'".

objective of the law is protection from any possible form of subjection, it may constitute a means of protection also of economic interests.[28]

Weber's idea of the relationship between law and economics is therefore merely coincidental; that is, it may arise by virtue of the specific objective which the law pursues, in other words, protection from abuse of power.

The structure of the relationship between economics and law is different: economic relations are based on the notion of reliance (the so-called "Interesse an der 'Verträgslegalität'), which translates into a complete faith placed by economic operators in the honesty of their interlocutors and in respecting agreements reached: "Die universelle Herrschaft der Markt vergesellschaftung verlangt einerseits ein anch rationalen Regeln kalkulierbares Funktionen des Rechts".[29]

Here is another observation made by Rebuffa regarding this topic: "At the beginning of the section of Economics and Society about the sociology of law, Weber tries to define the distinguishing features of public law and of private law: whilst public law regulates situations of authority, where "the holder of a dominant power faces other people… who are subordinate", the situations regulated by private law are those where "defining legal spheres is the legally correct meaning of the activity of the legislature, or of the judge or of the parties involved themselves […]".[30]

Private law in the modern state originates from the replacement of "privilege", in the sense of the definition, on the part of communities and private citizens, of subjective legal spheres, with the rules of the market, as regards private relations and relations with bureaucracy – the public administration – with the aim of guaranteeing the impartiality of public law choices. The "two great rationalising forces" (the market and the public administration) determine an equilibrium through the substitution of the logic of privilege with that of the formal legal equality of all individuals belonging to the community.

3. Market rules and public administration rules

It is now necessary therefore to focus our attention on the distinction between these two main spheres of law, public and private.

Chapter VII of *Wirtschaft und Gesellshaft* is on the subject of this distinction, and the study of so-called "Rechtssoziologie". Weber begins: "Die heutige Rechtstheorie und

28 M. Weber, *WG*, 182: "Das Recht […] garantiert keineswegs nur ökonomische, sondern allerverschiedensten Interessen, von den normalerweise elementarsten: Schutz rein persönlicher Sicherheit is zu rein ideellen Gütern wie die eigenen 'Ehre' und derjenigen göttlicher Mächte. Es garantiert vor allem auch politische, kirchliche, familiäre oder andere Autoritätsstellungen und überhaupt soziale Vorzugslagen aller Art, welche zwar in der mannigfachsten Beziehungen ökonomisch bedingt und relevant sei mögen, aber selbst nichts".
Oekonomisches und auch nichts notwendig oder vorwiegend aus ökonomischen Gründen Begehertes sind".

29 M. Weber, *WG*, 198.

30 G. Rebuffa, *Nel crepuscolo della democrazia cit.*, 100.

Rechtspraxis kennt als eine der wichtiges Scheidungen diejenige von 'öffentlichem' und 'Privatrecht'. Zwar über das Prinzip der Abgrenung herrscht Streit".

Once the difference between public law and private law has been identified, Weber strives to define the boundaries of the two systems. The operation, as Weber himself admitted, is anything but easy: "Auch heute also ist die Abgrenzung der Sphäre von öffentlichem und privaten Recht nicht überall eindutig".[31]

Public law is made up of the set of regulations (die Gesamheit der "Reglements") concerned with proceedings related to the institution of the State, actions which are needed to maintain, to extend and to directly pursue the State's objectives.

Private law is, on the contrary, concerned with actions regulated by the provisions of the State: "Mann könnte 'öffentliches' Recht identifizieren mit der Gesamtheit der 'Reglements', also: der ihrem richtigen juristichen Sinn nach nur Anweisungen an die Staatsorgane entalten den nicht aber erworbene subjektive Recht Einzelner begründenen Normen, im Gegensatz zu den 'Aus pruchsnormierungen', welche solche subjectiven Recht begründen".

The difficulty in pinpointing a precise demarcation line between the two spheres is principally due to the fact that one of the areas of regulatory jurisdiction of public players in the modern State is the area related to the distribution of economic commodities and of powers. Hence, tension is created between regulatory monopolisation and private autonomy that may cause unstable legitimacy of the political group which exercises regulatory powers monopolistically.

With the purpose of finding an equilibrium amongst such tension, it is necessary to ground all conflicts pertaining to goods and powers on predetermined procedures. They must, in other words, be "regulated". In this way, the rules of private law, exclusively based on criteria of formal and procedural justice, and that is to say on regulation aimed at safeguarding contractual autonomy, appear as the supporting structures of the legitimacy of the rational power of the modern State. Even though it is regulated, the activity of private law is considered as an expression of the rationality of the State rationality and, as such, may be exercised both by private and public players.

The state's system of private law, Rebuffa again observes in his discussion of Weber's reasoning, is hence formed as a structure which limits the powers of the political branch, removing discretionary power from it.[32]

A careful definition of jurisdiction constitutes then a guarantee that sovereignty will not become simply arbitrary, but, on the contrary, that it is channelled and directed within an organised system.

Sovereignty, the notion of *Herrschaft* which was mentioned above, must necessarily be connected (maybe even bound) to that of "Administration" (Herrschaft…mit Verwaltung verbunden ist), in the sense that it is an expression of, and is articulated in, the form of the administration. Likewise the administration is in need of sovereignty, since it is directed and organised in accordance with sovereignty's orders: "Herrschaft" interessiert uns hier in erster Linie, sofern mit "Verwaltung" verbunden ist jede Herrschaft

31 M. Weber, *WG*, 387.

32 G. Rebuffa, *Max Weber e la scienza del diritto cit.*, 103.

äußert sich und funktioniert als Verwaltung. Jede Verwaltung bedarf irgendwie der Herrschaft, denn immer müssen zu ihrer Führung irgendwelche Befehlesgewalten in irgend jemandes Hand gelegt sein".[33]

Thus, here is a definition that sees a reciprocal interrelation between sovereignty and public administration: if one thinks back to the line of argument that has been followed to reach such a conclusion, it is clear that it is an extremely linear process: from the individual to the collective, from the rules of economics to the rules of law, from the public and private distinction, the process of rationalisation follows a crescendo, a progression which rises in intensity, and that reaches its apex with the definition of the rules of good governance.

After having traced the relationship between *Herrschaft* and *Verwaltung*, Weber specifies that sovereignty must be exercised by means of an organized system: "Herrschaft durch 'organization' wie Struktur einer Herrschaft empfängt nun ihren soziologichen Charakter zunächst durch die allgemeine Eigenhart der Beziehung des oder der Herren zum der Apparat und beider zu den beherrschten und weiterhin durch die ihr spezifischen prinzipien der 'Organization'".

The correct application (die Geltung) of an order is expressed in a rational system of rules: "'Die Geltung' einer Befehlsgewalt kann ausgedrückt seine entweder in einem System gesatzer [...] rationalen Regeln". This passage is particularly important: "Der Gehorsam wird den Regeln, nicht der Person geleistet". It is a question of compliance with rules and not the person who makes them.

The rationalisation process here is at its highest expression: sovereignty as power exercised within an organized system of rules, endowed with intrinsic and cogent force and not, and no longer, sovereignty as an expression of personal will.

Weber then proceeds to list the principles that guarantee the correct operation of the public administration: the principle of competence (Kompetenz), according to which public action is performed by a body to which the power to exercise it (Behorde) has been conferred, or, as regards private action, by the offices (Bertriebes).[34]

Next is the principle of hierarchy (Amtshierarchie), according to which every administrative decision may be subject to the control of a body which is superordinate to the one which made the decision. It does not seem to be by chance that here a concept re-emerges which is very dear to Weber: Beruf, profession, intended as calling, or vocation: "Das Amt ist 'Beruf'".

Furthermore, public action must be characterised by the utmost technicism and endowed with the principles of precision, rapidity, correctness, efficiency, continuity, discretion, coherence and rationalisation: "Der entscheidende Grund für dar Vordringen der bürocratische Organisation war von jeher ihre rein techinische Überlegenheit über

33 M. Weber, *WG*, 345.

34 WG, 551 and ff.; and also p. 125: "die Grundkategorien der rationalen Herrschaft sind also: 1. ein kontinuierlicher regelgegundener Betrieb vom Amtsgeschäften, innerhalb: 2. eine Kompetenz (Zuständigkeit), welche bedeutet: a) einen kraft Leistungsverteilung sachlich abgegrensten Bereich von Leistungsplflichten – b) mit Zuordnung der etwa dafür erforderlichen Befehlsgewalten und c) mit fester Abgrenzung der eventuell zulässigen Zwangsmittel und der Voraussetzungen ihrer Anwendung. Ein derart geortneter Betrieb soll 'Behorde' heißen".

jede andere form. Ein voll entwickelter bürokratische Mechanismus verhält sich zu diese genau wie eine Maschine zu den nicht mechanischen Arten der Güternzeugung. Präzision, Schnelligkeit, Eindeutigkeit, Aktenkundigkeit, Kontinuierlichkeit, Diskretion, Einheitlichkeit, straffe Unterordnung".[35]

It is not difficult to notice the degree of influence that Weber's claims have exercised on the concept of the parcelling out of powers and likewise the modernity of a kind of thinking that dwells on the need to identify homogeneous criteria for the rules of private law and public law.

However, as has already been noted, Max Weber's thinking is also the product of his time, during which a rigid antinomy between public and private law existed.

As Cassese observes regarding this point: "Weber was probably influenced by the opinion, which was preponderant at the beginning of the 20th century, of separation between public and private, which were considered as two poles sustained by distinct rules and principles".[36]

As a result of the Frankfurt School and Habermas, it was possible to disengage such reflections from the legacy of the past, instilling in contemporary thought the idea of administration controlled by non-hierarchical power centres, not placed in the ideal pyramid that represented the unitary nature of the national order, but rather allocated according to a decentralised network system[37], organized in compliance with functional criteria.[38] Power, it has been said, is realised in the structures of an efficient administration, upheld by the principles mentioned above of continuity, competence, impartiality and hierarchy: "Ein derart geordneter Betrieb solls 'Behörde' heißen".

Maybe it is precisely in the notion of Behörde, intended as "Authority", that it may be possible to find a way towards resolving the previously mentioned dichotomy.

35 M. Weber, *WG*, 562. See D. Beetham, *Max Weber and the Theory of Modern Politics*, Polity Press, Cambridge, in association with Basic Blackwell, Oxford, 132, who observes how important was in Weber the idea of a bureaucracy technically efficient "first was his familiar conception of bureacracy as a technically efficient instrument of administration, technically the most perfectly adapted for achieving the highest level of performance". Secondly, bureaucracy is considered a separate power group "within the society, capable of influencing the goals and character of that society". Finally, bureaucracy as a mirror of the society: "far from embodying the universal and disinterested outlook ascribed to it by conservative mithology, in practice it was unable to free itself from the outlook of the social classes from which it was recruited and to which it was allied".

36 S. Cassese, *Lo spazio giuridico globale cit.*, 124: "Weber era probabilmente influenzato dall'opinione, prevalente all'inizio del XX secolo, della separazione tra pubblico e privato, considerati come due poli retti da principi e regole diversi".

37 S. Cassese, *La funzione costituzionale dei giudici non statali, dallo spazio giuridico globale all'ordine giuridico globale*, in *Riv. trim. dir. pubbl.*, 2007, 625.

38 T.W. Adorno, E. Fromm, M. Horkheimer, Löwenthal, H. Marcuse, F. Pollock, *La Scuola di Francoforte. La storia e i testi.* Introduzione e cura di E. Donaggio, Torino, 2005; J. P. McCormick, *Max Weber and Jürgen Habermas: The Sociology and Philosophy of Law During Crisis of the State*, in *Yale Journal of Law and Humanities*, 9, 1997, 297; E. Scheuerman, *Between the Norm and the Exception: The Frankfurt School and the Rule of Law*, Cambridge, 194; P.C. Caldwell, *Popular Sovereignty and the Crisis of German Constitutional Law: the Theory and Practice of Weimar Constitutionalism*, Durham, Duke University Press, 1997.

In Weber's writings understandably this new interpretation did not fully and completely develop. Nevertheless, there are traces in his work that may allow us to understand that he had the unquestionable merit of bringing to light the transversal meaning of the concept of "Authority": "'Behörden' in diesem Sinn gibt es in großen Privatbetrieben, Parteien, Armene naturlich genau wie in 'Staat' und 'Kirche'. Eine 'Behörde' im Sinne dieser terminologie ist auch der gewählte Staatspräsident (oder das Kollegium der Minister oder gewählten 'Volkbeauftragten')".

This definition brings us back, in a certain sense, to the purpose which was expressed at the opening pages of this dissertation; briefly it is the need to follow the development of the concept of authority, of public power, from the time of Weber's analysis to modern times. This may help us comprehend the dynamics which guided the process of formation of the European Community and which, as a consequence, have modified *radicitus* the approach of single member states in regard to public administration action.

In short we return to the theme, previously outlined, of fragmentation of power, its decentralization, and its channelling into institutions functionally assigned to the protection of the so-called "sensitive sectors".

The wave of sovereignty, weakened by the strength of the sea, by the 20th century's history of crisis, breaks and changes its structure.

While emphasising the indispensable function of the bureaucratic apparatus in the rule of law, Max Weber did, however, give warning of the risk of an excess of power in administrative action: He asked himself what measures could work to keep such a tendency under control: "Die rein bureaukratische, also: die bureaukratisch-monokratische aktenmäßige Verwaltung ist nach aalen Erfahrungen die an Präzision, Stetigkeit, Disziplin, Straffheit und Verläßlikeit".

A first approximate answer to the problem of guaranteeing the "purity" (die Reinheit) of an efficient democracy lies in the level of competence and effectiveness that the public bodies manage to achieve, competence which is naturally measured by the degree of responsibility which they are willing to take.

"How to keep the bureaucracy subject to political control" scholars of Weberian philosophy often wonder. Probably by means of a combination between passion and vocation: "In 'Politics as a Vocation' Weber defined the qualities necessary to this type (that is of the 'model politician', who directly accepts responsibility for his actions) as a combination of passion with 'Sachlichkeit': the determination to fight for a cause he believed in, combined with a very practical and down-to-earth knowledge of the means by which it could be attained".

The legacy that Weber left for those who came after him thus are, essentially, questions as to which elements are capable of rendering democracy stable and of safeguarding rationality. If individual responsibility is fundamental in the building of a democratic system, it will be necessary to give voice to individuals, in order to help them fully express their vocation.

4. Max Weber's legacy in contemporary philosophical and legal thinking

We have taken as our distant starting point the year 1950, in order to identify how the proposal to pool coal and steel resources at a European level was determined by deeper motivations than the simple economic interests that the member states wished to pursue.

In this regard the following observation of Tommaso Padoa Schioppa is relevant: "The process of European integration is the most powerful positive legacy that this century has left to humankind in the area of political organisations. It shows that human society can, through peaceful means, evolve from the rule of nature to civilization, even in a field – relations between sovereign States – in which that transition had never been possible [...]".[39]

It is now necessary to follow the developments after the creation of the system theorised by Weber, in search of those cardinal points which have guided the States in the formation of the European system, following Weber's queries concerning the legitimacy of power "in the light of the growth of the administrative state".[40]

From the start, it seems auspicious to be following the footsteps of those who have identified as the ultimate objective the achievement of the Kantian goal of perpetual peace, seeing this as the first and foremost political lesson to be drawn from European history in the past 50 years: "If there is a duty, and if together with this duty there exists a solid hope of making possible the rule of public law, albeit in a gradual movement towards the infinite, then *perpetual peace*, which follows what have been so far referred to as peace treaties (but in actuality are only armistices), is not a hollow idea, but a task that, accomplished little by little, draws ever closer to its aim (given that the timeframe in which such progress is accomplished will hopefully become shorter and shorter)".[41]

While the objective of perpetual peace may appear to be almost a visionary's dream, it nevertheless remains of the utmost importance in order to comprehend Habermas' ideas, which gave new impetus to the shared desire of European States to establish peaceful relations among themselves. It is possible to reach perpetual peace only if States agree to limit their sovereign power, establishing an organisation which is not based on

39 T. Padoa Schioppa, *Europa, forza gentile. Cosa ci ha insegnato l'avventura europea*, Bologna, 2001, 13: "Il processo di unificazione europea è la più forte eredità positiva che il secolo lascia agli uomini nella sfera degli ordinamenti politici. È la dimostrazione che la società umana può, con mezzi pacifici, passare dallo Stato di natura alla civiltà, anche in un campo – i rapporti tra Stati sovrani – nel quale quell passaggio non era ancora riuscito [...]".

40 D. Dyzenhaus, *The Legitimacy of Legality*, in *Archiv für Rechts- und Sozialphilosophie (ARSP)*, vol. 82, 1996, Heft 1, 326: "Max Weber set the stage for debate on both the nature of law and the separation of powers by stating a powerful case for a connection between these issues".

41 I. Kant, *Per la pace perpetua*, pref. by S. Veca, it. transl. by R. Bordiga, XII ed., Milano, 2005. I. Kant, *Zum ewigen Frieden. Ein philosophischer Entwurf*, 1795, in *Kant gesammelte Schriften, hrsg. von der Königlich Preußischen*, Akademie der Wissenschaften, Berlin Leipzig, 1900, vol. VII, 1912. See also J. Habermas, "*Kants Idee des Ewigen Friedens – aus dem Historischem Abstand von 200 Jahren*", KJ, 1995, 301 V. Gerhardt, *Immanuel Kants entwurf "Zum Ewigen Frieden", Eine Teorie der Politik*, Wissenschftliche Buchgesellschaft Damrstadt, 1995. R. Alexy, *Basic Rights and Democracy in Habermas's Procedural Paradigm of the Law*, in *Ratio Juris*, n. 2, 1994; N. Bobbio, *Scienza del diritto ed analisi del linguaggio* (1950), in *Diritto e analisi del linguaggio*, cur. by U. Scarpelli, Edizioni Comunità, Milano, 1976; see also W. Penn, *Essai d'un projet pour rendre la paix de l'Europe solide et durable*, Williams Sessions, The Ebor Press, York, England, 1986; H. Klenner, *Kants Entwurf "Zu ewigen Frieden" – Illusion oder Utopie?*, in *Archiv für Rechts- und Sozialphilosophie (ARSP)*, vol. 82, 1996, Heft 1, 152.

the power of a single individual, but on that of the whole community, conceiving a federation that is a pact (*foedus*) between citizens of the world rather than a pact between States: "Die Außere Souveränität der Staaten sei dergestalt zu limitieren, daß Deren Wechselbeziehungen zu einem Innerverhältnis von Organisationsmitgliedern bei einem Gewaltmonopol der Völkergemeinschaft modifiziert werden; die weltbürgerliche Vereinigung sei weniger als eine Föderation von Staaten, vielmehr als eine Föderation von Weltbürgern zu konzipieren".[42]

It only remains, therefore, to explore the thinking of those who have strived in the endeavour to accomplish such a noble cause.

4.1. Jurgen Habermas: "the German respondent to Max Weber"[43]

As previously stated, one of the unresolved questions of Weber's theories related to the principle of legitimacy of the power-holder, who, by taking responsibility for his own actions, should guarantee fulfilment of the expectations of single individuals and of the community, who have placed their total trust in him. In Europe, the practical effects of the inability to overcome the obstacle of the danger of abuse of power by an individual, by means of subversion of power, are, sadly, well known: "This subversion from within ended in Germany in Nazism; and Habermas has made an important political contribution to German public life in his critique of the remnants of the unreason of Nazism in German public life".[44]

In essence, the basic theoretical difficulty always seems to be the principle of democratic legitimacy. Is it possible, in other words, to guarantee that the choices of the person to whom power has been conferred by the will of the people are actually an expression of this will? And are the population permitted to express, in some manner, their dissent?

Using J. McCormick's effective image, it may be said that the ghost of the failure of the Weimar Republic, on whose establishment much of Weber's effort was spent, long haunted Habermas and greatly influenced his thinking: "I will argue here that in order to fully understand Habermas's theoretical efforts [...] one must take into account the legal sociological framework that he inherits from Max Weber. This is by no means a purely intellectual or cultural inheritance, for Weber's sociology of law played a crucial role in the historical drama that was the collapse of Germany's first effort at liberal and social democracy: the Weimar Republic. It is the ghost of this failure that has haunted virtually all of Habermas's theoretical endeavours".[45]

42 J. HABERMAS, in the speech reported by H. KLENNER, *Kants Entwurf "Zum ewigen Frieden" – Illusion oder Utopie? cit.*, 159.

43 D. DYZENHAUS, *The legitimacy of Legality cit.*, 327.

44 Again D. DYZENHAUS, *op. ult. cit.*, 327.

45 J.P. MCCORMICK, *Max Weber and Jürgen Habermas: the Sociology and Philosophy of Law During Crises of the State*, in *Yale Journal of Law and the Humanities*, 1997, 9, 298: "I claim that Habermas's textual and often subtextual desire to address those legal-theoretical problems that confronted Weber in a particular crisis of the state at the dawn of this century significantly undermines his attempt to address contemporary socio-political concerns. There exists a qualitatively different crisis of the state, and the

Habermas begins with the assumption, dear to Weber, of the need for rationalisation and "disenchantment of the world": "the fate of our times is characterized by rationalization and intellectualization and, above all, by the 'disenchantment of the world'".[46]

In particular, in *Theory of Communicative Action*, starting from the sociologists who preceded him (Weber *in primis*)[47], and examining Weber's notion of rational action, and specifically of rational action as regards value, Habermas transposes this theory, relating it to social interaction mediated by language.

The analysis of two experts on Habermas is interesting in this regard: "the process of discourse itself is inevitably dispersed across a variety of *fora*: these include face-to-face interactions at home and at work; larger meetings in the various informal voluntary associations and different levels of organization throughout civil society [...]; the dissemination of information and arguments through the public media; and the complex network of governing institutions, agencies, and decision-making bodies".[48]

role of law within it, at the twilight of the twentieth-century than that in effect in Weber's time. The legal crisis with which Weber dealt was influenced in large part by the transition from a nineteenth-century non-interventionist state model to a twentieth century welfare-state one, and the present predicament of law and the state is increasingly generated by transitional phenomena associated with growing interdependence of nation states". See also D. Dayzenhaus, *Legality and legitimacy. Carl Schmitt, Hans Kelsen and Hermann Heller in Weimar*, Clarendon Pres, Oxford, 1997, in part. p. 236 and ff.: "He [Habermas] also wants to respond to Weber's account of law and politics, since, in his view, that account helped to undermine the role of legal order as a potential bulwark against the Nazi seizure of power"; e ancora: "In 1964 at a conference held in Heidelberg to commemorate the centenary of Weber's birth, Habermas pointed out that an evaluation of Weber from the German point of view had to be very different from the 'liberal' interpretation that Weber's work had received in America. For, Habermas maintained, in Germany Weber's political sociology, in particular the 'decisionist element' therein, had a 'different history' in its consequences in the Weimar period. In particular, he alleged "If we are to judge Weber here and now, we cannot overlook the fact that Carl Schmitt was a 'legitimate pupil' of Weber's". Id., *The Legitimacy of Legality*, University of Toronto Law Journal, 46, 1996; C.R. Sunstein, *Democracy Isn't What You Think*, *New York Times Book Review*, 18 August 1996; M. Rosenfeld, *Law as a Discourse: Between Democracy and Rights*, *Harvard Law Review*, 108, 1995, J. Bohman, *Complexity, Pluralism and the Constitutional State*, *Law and Society Review*, 28, 1994, D. Rasmussen, *How is Valid Law Possible?*, *Philosophy and Social Criticism*, 20, 1994.

46 D. Dyzenhaus, *Legality and Legitimacy cit.*, 236.

47 J. Habermas, *Discourse Ethics: Notes on a Program of Philosophical Justification*, Cambridge, MIT Press, 1990, 65. Id., *Faktizität und Geltung: Beiträge zur Diskurstheorie des Rechts und des demokratischen Rechtstaats*, Frankfurt am Main, Suhrkamp, 192; *Between facts and norms*, transl. by W. Rehg, published by MIT Press, 1996, 111: "Equal participation of all who are affected; the postulate of unlimitedness, i.e. the fundamental unboundedness and openness concerning time and persons; the postulate of freedom from constraint (*Zwangslosigkeit*), i.e., the freedom, in principle, of discourse from accidental and structural forms of power; and the postulate of seriousness or authenticity (*Ernsthaftigkeit*), i.e., the absence of deception and even illusion in expressing intentions and in performing speech acts".

48 W. Rehg e J. Bohman, *Discourse and Democracy: The Formal and Informal Bases of Legitimacy in* Between Facts and Norms, in R. Von Schomberg and K. Baynes (ed.), *Discourse and democracy. Essays on Habermas's Between Facts and Norms*, State University of New York Press, New York, 2002, 31, in part. 37: "*The facts of complexity* seem to present deliberative democracy with a Weberian dilemma: either the decisionmaking institutions gain effectiveness at the cost of democratic deliberation, or they retain democracy at the cost of effective decision making".

It is the communication between social actors which produces adherence to values, and common opinions and practices: "Firstly, I do not assert that humankind wishes to act communicatively but that humankind is obliged to do so. When parents educate their offspring, when the current generation takes possession of the knowledge passed down from previous ones, when individuals and groups cooperate, in other words they desire to live peacefully without resorting to a measure as costly as the use of force, they are obliged to act communicatively. There are elementary functions of society which may be assured only by acting communicatively".[49]

In communicative action language is aimed at conveying the truth and is targeted towards comprehension, consensus and the exchange of viewpoints and views of the world; it is precisely on the basis of communicative action that Habermas establishes a theory of democracy centred on dialogue, propounding a way for a possible connection between communicative action and the problems associated with democratic legitimacy. The words of Habermas clearly resound once again: "I call communicative those interactions in which participants coordinate their plans of action in common agreement; the agreement which is reached on each occasion is proportionate to the players' recognition of their claims of validity".[50]

The legitimacy of the agreement is achieved because of mutual recognition by players of its internal coherence, in other words of its validity. Agreement amongst a number of individuals in the pursuit of particular objectives and the use of certain means to attain them is the result of a communicative process, during which every individual advances claims of validity for their own proposals: from the interweaving (network) and juxtaposition of the arguments adopted in support of such claims, mutual recognition of the valid proposal to be adopted by common consent is attained.

With this idea Habermas makes an opening towards the possibility of democratic legitimacy of decisions of public interest, because of the achievement of a consensus which is expressed in a valid manner. In one particular passage Weber's aporia regarding the impossibility of finding a legitimate foundation for the exercise of power seems to be completely resolved: "The separation from normative contexts and the distance of communicative action from institutions based on tradition, in other words from the yoke of consensus, weighs on (overburdening it) the mechanism of agreement, implying an increasing requirement for coordination. On the other hand [...], in place of institutions, 'bodies' and other new types of organizations emerge; they are formed on the basis of communication *media* that detach action from processes of understanding, coordinating it by the use of generalised instruments such as power or money. These *media* of control establish language as a mechanism controlling actions".[51]

Discourse is therefore structured between new types of players and

49 J. Habermas, *Dopo l'utopia. Il pensiero critico e il mondo d'oggi* interviewed by Michael Haller. Ed. by W. Privitera, with an updating on postcomunism, Venezia, 1992, 113.

50 J. Habermas, *Etica del discorso*, by E. Agazzi, Roma-Bari, 1989, 66.

51 J. Habermas, *Teoria dell'agire comunicativo cit.*, I, 460. About the connections between Weber and habermas see S. Costantino, *Sfere di legittimità e processi di legittimazione. Weber, Schmitt, Luhmann, Habermas*, Torino, 1994.

organisations, that, through the use of language, develop forms of cooperation and take "shared" decisions.

Consequently, it is not sufficient for the validity of a rule to be individually accepted, that is to say, through the reasoning that each individual has with himself: it is necessary, instead, for recognition to depend on mutual agreement between players.[52]

The model expounded by Habermas is without any doubt fascinating and to a certain extent indispensable in order to arrive at an idea of legitimacy of power which is not reached through imposition from above, but by means of an egalitarian exchange of information. And this model seems to complete Weber's theories in a worthy manner, coinciding with the notion that the exercise of sovereignty needs to be represented by a new geometrical figure: not a pyramid, but rather a network. In this system, once again, as with Weber, the model of a market economy may serve as a guide in the search for an effective fulfilment of democratic needs: "The markets, which cannot be made democratic on a par with state administrations, increasingly adopt a function of guidance in areas of life that, up to now, have been held together in a regulatory manner, either politically or through the use of pre-political forms of communication. Thus the polarisation of private spheres is increasingly turned towards mechanisms of action oriented towards success and respective preferences, but the domain subject to the public constraints of legitimacy is also decreasing".[53]

The image of the network in which the exchange of consensus is accomplished can help to obviate the pitfalls in which a non-participatory democracy may fall, provided, however, that it does not turn into a dangerous "virtual trap", confined to the realm of ideas.

On this subject, the words spring to mind of one who, although with a hint of pessimism, compared the legal system to the rules used in the game of chess: "There is no doubt whatsoever that the individual players that constitute the political community may be considered similar to the pieces in a game of chess [ ]. However it would be completely mistaken and thus disastrous also from the purely operative point of view [ ] to presume that human playerss move like chess pieces, that is, due to the intervention of an external and superimposed will, and not, as in experience, which is the only reality within reach of mankind, due to an autonomous decision, of which one must take account".[54]

52 It is the so called: "*Wir-Perspektive*", taken by R.B. Brandom, *Making it Explicit*, Cambridge (Mass.), 1994, 5: "The most cosmopolitan approach begins with a pluralist insight. When we ask, Who are we? Or What sort of thing are we? The answers can vary without competing. Each one defines a different way of saying 'we'; each kind of 'we' saying defines a different community. It points to the one great Community comprising members of all particular communities – the Community of those who say 'we' with and to someone, whether the members of those different communities recognize each other or not". Diese große C – osserva Habermas – könnte den idealen Bezugspunkt für die rationale Akzeptabilität jener unbedingten, d.h. kontexttranszendirenden Geltungssprüche bezeichnen, die sich vor einem "immer weiteren" Publikum rechtfertigen lassen müssen. J. Habermas, *Kommunikatives Handeln und detranszendentalisierte Vernunft*, Philipp Reclam jun. Stuttgart, 2001, 80.

53 J. Habermas, *Tra scienza e fede*, transl. it. by Mario Carpitella, Roma-Bari, 2006, 11.

54 F. Gentile, *Ordinamento giuridico tra virtualità e realtà*, in U. Pagallo, *Testi e contesti dell'ordinamento giuridico*, Padova, 1999, 217.

The comparison is certainly appealing: below we will see how it perfectly fits the controversial aspect of abandoning sovereignty imposed "from above", and the new criteria that must be followed in order to guarantee good governance.

5. The legal world as a chessboard

The game of chess. Pawns, knight, bishop, rook, queen and king. They all move on the same board, in the same network. The first are less easily manoeuvrable than the others, but are not, for this reason, subordinated to the latter; each piece follows the rules which were defined beforehand and accepted by all. The hierarchical pyramid is displaced by the reticular chessboard. Cassese's warning resounds imperiously. "Those who venture into this problem area must abandon the hierarchical view of legal systems and forget the idea of stratified levels: the links between the various levels are unpredictable".[55]

Sovereignty (that very concept in which, however, Weber, it must be remembered, had sensed a "transversal" nature) is interpreted in a new way, structuring itself within a network system: "die Netzmetaphor ist augenscheinlich vieldeutig, ihr entescheidendes Charakteristikun für den rechtswissenschaftlichen Gebrauch besteht aber darin, dass bestimmte in den Rechtswissenschaften gebräuchliche Unterscheidungen durch sie unterlaufen werden".[56]

The model of "reticular" collaboration consists of a system in which the dynamics between administrative bodies are resolved via interdependent and non-hierarchical relations: "A set of relatively stable relationships which are non-hierarchical and of interdependent nature between a variety of corporate actors".[57]

Furthermore, at least five distinctive characteristics of a reticular organization may be identified:

1. The concept of *network* expresses in itself a dual essence, one related to private law and one to public law;
2. The level of cooperation which it produces appears to be devoid of any institutionalisation whatsoever;
3. One of the most important factors consists in the methods of interconnection between the authorities which operate within this system, since they are the ganglions from which its nerves depart;

55 S. CASSESE, *Diritto amministrativo europeo e diritto amministrativo nazionale: signoria o integrazione?*, in *Riv. it. dir. pubbl. com.*, 2004, 1136: "Chi si inoltri in questa problematica, deve abbandonare la concezione gerarchica degli ordini giuridici e dimenticare l'idea di una stratificazione di livelli: i legami tra le diverse parti sono irregolari".

56 C. MÖLLERS, *Transnationale Behördenkooperation cit.*, 371; ID., *Netzwerk als Kategorie des Organisationsrechts*, in J. OEBBECKE (ed.), *Dezentrale nicht-normative Steuerung*, 2005; C. JOERGES, K.H. LADEUR, E. VOS (eds), *Integrating Scientific Expertise into Regulatory Decision Making*, 1997; R. WOLFRUM *Vorbeitende Willensbildung und Entscheidungsprozeß beim Abschluß multilateral völkerrechtlicher Verträge*, FS Rauschning, 2001.

57 BÖRZEL, *Policy Networks – A New Paradigm of European Governance?*, EUI Working Papers, RSC 97/19, 1997, 5; E. CHITI, *The Emergence of a Community Administration: the case of European Agencies*, in *Common Market Law Review*, 2000, 339.

4. The institutions themselves have a role of mediation between the operators of the system;
5. The system becomes, in its turn, the source and model of reference suited to ensuring an efficient exchange of information and to developing new behavioural standards.[58] Such a system however is not always suited to satisfying the need for dialogue between the market's operators.

The more players recognise themselves in the system of rules, the more the rules are predefined, clear and above all homogeneous. The rules become a seismograph measuring relationships between players, and recording alterations. From the impact they have on those they are intended for an effective picture can be obtained of the wellbeing of the system: the law, in which the rules acquire formal expression, becomes "a sort of sensitive seismograph, set close to the conflicts, yielding rich, even if often encoded, messages from 'reality'".[59]

The rules which determine uniform *standards* become in that sense a crucial element of cooperation between systems[60]: "under conditions of reasonable pluralism, the law is required to dampen conflict and promote efficacious problem solving, absent a unitary (coercive) sovereign. In contrast to other institutions, however, law must find the answers to this challenge with a careful eye to the maintenance of its own normative coherence".[61]

58 E. Chiti, *The Emergence of a Community cit.*, 329: "The concept of network, as elaborated by a rich literature, is a powerful analytical instrument. [...] First, the concept of network usually refers to an organization including both public and private bodies. Second, it indicates forms of co-operation with a low level of institutionalization; certain studies, in particular, highlight the prevalence of interpersonal relationships over the relations between bodies and institutions. Third, the literature on policy networks emphazises the relevance of the 'links' between the various bodies [...]; fourth, some scholars conceptualize the networks as "institutions, that is as sets of rules [...] regulating the interactions among the subjects, limiting their options and providing them with specific opportunities. Fifth, a number of particularly important studies directly dedicated to European agencies, highlight the learning process which takes place through the networks; the networks function, thus, is not only to permit an efficient division of labour and the exchange of information or other resources, but also to facilitate the development of behavioural standards and working practices that create shared expectations and enhance the effectiveness of the social mechanisms of reputational enforcement".

59 C. Joerges, *"Deliberative Supranationalism" – Two Defences*, in *European Law Journal*, 2002, 133, 134. P. Kirchhof, *Der deutsche Staat im Prozeß der Europäischen Integration*, in J. Isensee, P. Kirchhof (eds.), *Handbuch des Staatsrechts der Bundesrepublik Deutschland*, Bd. VII, Heidelberg, 1992, 855. B. Kohler-Koch, *The Evolution and Transformation of European Governance*, in Kohler-Koch, Beate, Eising, Rainer (eds.), *The Transformation of Governance in the European Union*, London/New York, 1999, 14; K.H. Ladeur, *Die Autonomie der Bundesbank – ein Beispiel für die institutionelle* Verarbeitung von Ungewißheitsbedingungen, Staatswissenschaften und Staatspraxis 4, 1993, 486, ID., Das Umweltrecht der Wissensgesellschaft, Berlin, 1995; ID., Towards a Legal Theory of Supranationality: The Viability of the Network Concept, European Law Journal, 1997, 33.

60 E.D. Kidney, *The Emerging Field of International Administrative Law and Justice Working Papers*, 2001, 1; C. Möllers, *Internationales Verwltungsrecht*, 2005; ID., *Verfassunggebende Gewalt – Verfassung – Konstitutiolisierung*, in A.V. Bogdandy, *Europäisches Verfassungsrecht*, 2003, 50.

61 C. Joerges, *"Deliberative Supranationalism" cit.*, 155, che aggiunge: *"In this context and in this sense, I have also repeatedly talked of 'good governance', particularly because the term* 'Verwaltung'

6. The new model of reticular cooperation in the European system

After this discussion of issues, from the historical and philosophical origins of a new approach to sovereignty, to the introduction of new models of cooperation, we return to the initial purpose of trying to understand the reasons underlying the establishment of new infranational and supranational power centres, distinguished primarily by a tutelary function of the sensitive areas of the system and equipped with specific technical competencies.

We started from the origins of the community system, which arose on primarily economic foundations, to then follow the progressive emergence of third party bodies with regard to the single States, and the various stages on the way towards a new vision of sovereignty.

It is now necessary to understand which tendencies exist in Europe today, in order to contextualise the activities of these agencies, and understand the roles they play and the influence they have on the systems of the single member States.[62]

(administration) does not capture that (inter-) governative element that is essential to the management of the Internal Market, because the formula of 'good' governance at least expresses a normative claim intended to raise gover*nance in the Internal Market above mere strategic negotiation-though, admittedly, without claiming to decipher conclusively the metaphor of good governance, and/or Ambrogio Lorenzetti's famous picture*". ID., "*Good Governance*" *in the European Internal Market: Two Competing Legal Conceptualisations of European Integration and their Synthesis*, in A. v. BOGDANDY, Y. MÉNY, P. MAVROIDES (eds.), *European Integration and International Co-Ordination. Studies in Transnational Economic Law – Liber Amicorum Claus-Dieter Ehlermann*, Kluwer, 2002, 219; C. JOERGES, F. RÖDL, "*Social Market Economy*" *as Europe's Social Model?*, EUI Working Paper, 2004, 8; ID., *Wurde Europa ein Großraum? Zäsuren, Kontinuitäten, Re-Konfigurationen in der rechtlichen Konzeptualisierung des Integrationsprojekts*, in MARKUS JACHETENFUCHS/MICHÈLE KNODT (eds.), *Regieren in internationalen Institutionen*, Oplad, 2002, 53–78; C. JOERGES, J. NEYER, *Von intergouvernementalem Bargaining zur deliberativen Politik: Gründe und Chancen für eine Konstitutionalisierung der europäischen Komitologie*, in: Beate Kohler-Koch (ed.), *Regieren in entgrenzten Räumen*, PVS-Sonderheft 28, Opladen, 1998, 207. C. JOERGES, J. FALKE (eds.), *Das Ausschußwesen der Europäischen Union. Die Praxis der Risikoregulierung im Binnenmarkt und ihre rechtliche Verfassung*, Baden-Baden, 2000; C. JOERGES, Y. MÉNY, J.H.H. WEILER (eds.), *What Kind of Constitution for What Kind of Polity? Responses to Joschka Fischer, Florence-Cambridge*, Mass.: Robert Schuman Centre/Jean Monnet Chair Harvard Law School, see also www.iue.it/RSC/symposium/, 2000. G. MAJONE, *The European Community. An "Independent Fourth Branch of Government?"*, in G. BRÜGGEMEIER (ed.), *Verfassungen für ein ziviles Europa*, Baden-Baden, 1994, 23; F. MAYER, *Die drei Dimensionen der Europäischen Kompetenzdebatte, Zeitschrift für ausländisches öffentliches Recht und Völkerrecht*, 2001, 577; E.J. MESTMÄCKER, *Auf dem Wege zu einer Ordnungspolitik für Europa*, in E.J. MESTMÄCKER, H. MÖLLER, H.P. SCHWARTZ (eds.), *Eine Ordnungspolitik für Europa. Festschrift für Hans v.d. Groeben*, Baden-Baden, 1997, 9; I. PERNICE, *Maastricht, Staat und Demokratie, Die Verwaltung* 26, 1993, 449.

62 P. KOSLOWSKI, *Market and Democracy as Discourses. Limits to Discoursive Social Coordination*, in ID. (ed.), *Individual Liberty and Democratic Decision-Making. The Ethics, Economics, and Politics of Democracy*, J.C.B. Mohr (Paul Siebeck), Tübingen 1987, 59: "Democratic market societies control their economics through the decision making process of the market and the coordinative process of the price system. Their political systems are guided by the voting process and the coordinative process of participatory formation of a common will. The market and the democracy are individualistic-discoursive decision-making systems which make decisions involving the economy and politics (individual and social choice) in accordance with individual preferences or statement of opinion of

The first problem to deal with is, in a sense, associated with the previously discussed need to harmonise, by means of the establishment of a core of common rules in which citizens and institutions may all recognise themselves and within which they may operate. It is essential not to forget the fundamental role that democratic principles have within the European Community, leaving aside any doubts which have been raised as regards its effectiveness.[63]

It is necessary to understand if agencies can act as a good link, not only to start up new forms of cooperation, but also to reconstruct the connective tissue where it may have become slack or even torn[64]; in other words, if the agencies themselves, or the citizens through them, may be considered to be a good sounding board for democratic and participatory needs, within that process of formation of will, which Habermas called "communicative action".

C. Harlow looked at the difficulties associated with the establishment of a system in which democratic aspirations may be fully achieved (and hence at the need to face the problem through the use of agencies): "[...] the EC professes democracy without being democratic. Thus the fragility of its political institutions, inherently perilous, necessarily reflects on the legitimacy of its legal order, while the constitutional balance intrinsic to the separation of powers ideal is dangerously absent. In other words, while in every Member State the administration law system forms part of a working system, this is not the case in the Community".[65]

both consumers ('consumer sovereignty') and the voters ('sovereignty of the people'). The market and democracy necessarily refer to one another in their common goal of discoursive mediation between individual freedom of choice and general social-political choice See *amplius* A. von Bogdandy, J.H.H. Weiler (eds.), *European Integration – The New German Scholarship*, with contribution by A. von Bogdandy; R. Ürpmann; F. Mayer; S. Kadelbach; J. Bast; A. Wiener, N. Walker; W. Schroeder; R.A. Wessel; M. Wagner (assoc. ed.), in Jean Monnet Working Paper 9/03.1.

63 A. Peters, *European Democracy after the 2003 Convention*, in *Common Market Law Review*, 2004, 41, 69, note 120. On that troubled matter that is the future of democracy, see the Council of Europe Publication: "*The future of democracy in Europe. Trends, analyses and reforms*", coordinated by P.C. Schmitter, and A.H. Trechsel, Council of Europe Publishing, Belgium, 2004. In the introductory remarks there is an explicit reference to Popper: "Democracy is the word for something that does not exist: "For something that does not exist, democracy has certainly been much talked about recently. Moreover – at least in Europe – 'real-existing' democracy seems to have a promising future, although it is currently facing an unprecedented diversity of challenges and opportunities. The issue is not whether the national, sub-national and supranational polities that compose Europe will become or remain democratic, but whether the quality of this regional network of democracies will suffice to ensure the voluntary support and legitimate compliance of its citizens. For there is abundant evidence that the citizens of Europe – while they may not agree on its existent practices or even know what 'it' really is – will not tolerate non-democracy".

64 D. Beach, *The Dynamic of European Integration. Why and when EU institutions matter*, The European Union Series, London, 2005, 258: "[...] the Constitutional Treaty is much clearer and simpler [than the existing treaties], which could have the disadvantage of providing strong ammunition to Eurosceptics and opponents in coming referendums. This is the democratic paradox of the treaty reform process, and could perhaps prove to be the Achilles heel of the Convention method".

65 C. Harlow, *European Administrative Law and the Global Challenge*, in P. Craig, G. De Búrca (ed.), *The evolution of EU Law*, Oxford University Press, 1999, 266.

Although Europe was born from a common sentiment of the countries that belong to it, today it is undeniably pervaded by various trends and changes: "the first reflects the internationalisation or globalisation of government in certain spheres, with an increasing number of issues being allocated to or addressed by international and supranational levels of authority; [...] a second trend at least within western political systems is that localisation, in the sense of emergence of stronger local and regional politics, with a renewed interest in more direct democratic participation under the influence of republican and communitarian political theories".[66]

The first trend arises from the need for internationalisation or intergovernmental globalisation, with the establishment of the so-called "global legal space", whose characteristics are clearly listed by Cassese: "Firstly there is a legal space, meaning the elimination of barriers (especially in the economic and financial field) [...] Secondly, among the secondary legal systems, (the national ones) there still persist strong differences, despite the continuing process of standardisation applied by the global legal order".[67]

The pressures which the national systems exert towards separatist needs constitute therefore the second problematic aspect, the second counter-thrust to the process of construction of Community law. This also brings resurgence of phenomena linked to particularism and affirmation of national sovereignty.

Finally, the third phenomenon is more hidden and its course is less predictable: the breaking down of the barriers between public and private, of that distinction which had been the basis of Weber's view of modern society: "it concerns the evolution [...] of a concept of governance which transcends the more traditionally conceived private/public divide and which challenges previous [...] assumptions about the locus of political and economic authority".[68]

These three trends provide the cast on which agencies model themselves. They aspire to satisfy the needs of internationalisation, but also to enhance the particularistic autonomy of the States and of interest groups (competition, protection of privacy, as well as financial, banking and insurance supervision, and so on).

For these reasons, before examining in detail the duties and functions assigned to them, it seems necessary to shed some light on the above-mentioned trend towards globalisation, since the other two trends, namely the protection of "particularistic" interests and the weakening of the distinction between public and private, will be examined in greater detail when we look at the individual authorities.

66 G. De Búrca, *Reappraising Subsidiarity's Significance after Amsterdam*, Harvard Jean Monnet Working Paper, 7/99, Harvard Law School Cambridge, 2000, 2.

67 S. Cassese, *Lo spazio giuridico globale cit.*, 17. See also B. Carotti, L. Casini, *Diritto amministrativo globale*. Bibliografia, in S. Cassese, M. Conticelli (eds.), *Diritto e amministrazioni nello spazio giuridico globale*, Quaderni della Rivista trimestrale di dir. pubblico, Milano, 2006, 301. regarding the problems of global trade see M. Fusaro, *Reti commerciali e traffici globali in età moderna*, Bari, 2008.

68 G. De Búrca, *Reappraising Subsidiarity's Significance after Amsterdam*, Harvard Jean Monnet Working Paper, 7/99 *cit.*, 3.

6.1. Globalisation

Globalisation. The use of the word "globe" may be traced back to the 16th century, when Magellan circumnavigated the earth and thus proved it to be a sphere.

The expression "global village" was first used by Marshall McLuhan, a scholar of mass communication, in 1964, in his book in which he analysed the effects that each "medium" or technology had, during the transition from the mechanical to the electric era and just before the electronic age, on changes in our way or life: "We live mythically and integrally [...] in the electric age, when our central nervous system is technologically extended to involve in the whole of mankind and to incorporate the whole of mankind in us, we necessarily participate [...] in the consequences of our every action".[69]

The new world which emerged in the 20th century is, according to McLuhan, distinguished by decentralisation, that shifts the primary point of interest and observation (and of finalization) from a subjective viewpoint in the village dimension, to an impersonal global viewpoint: "As electrically contracted, the globe is no more than a village. Electric speed at bringing all social and political functions together in a sudden implosion has heightened human awareness of responsibility to an intense degree".[70] The global village is a beautifully fitting oxymoron, suggesting that the community, united by the speed of trade and communication, takes on the dimensions of a village. This expression became extremely widespread with the emergence of new technologies (first and foremost the internet, and here the idea reappears of communication through a reticular or network system). In this sense, it may be applied both to describe how the huge world has shrunk to an easily explored domain similar to a village, and also to indicate how each village within the world has destroyed its borders. The words "globalisation and globalise" only appeared in academic language from the mid 1980s.[71]

The world has become a global area, where players, be they individuals or communities, interact free of the barriers of territorial borders.

They exercise their choices without any limits.

European society is, in fact, a society of *individuals*, that portray themselves as "*Marktbürger*" – with echoes of Weber – or simple citizens in a supranational public place, perceived as an extension of the private domain.

Nations, like individuals, do likewise.

Hence the future of globalization depends on the skill of both individuals and nations in contributing to the opening up of choices and of integration.

Once again, Cassese's considerations are enlightening: "Once the existence of a superior authority has been excluded, on which a hierarchy of bodies depends, and when the existence of all the elements of an international legal order have been recognised, assuming that the latter exhibits a complex organisation, without, however, having a

69 M. McLuhan, *Gli strumenti del comunicare*, Milano, 2002; M. McLuhan, L. Lapham, *Understanding Media: The Extensions of Man*, ed. W. Terrence Gordon, 1964, nuova ed. 2003.

70 M. McLuhan, *The Extensions of a Man cit.*, 5.

71 H. Shams, *Law in the Context of "Globalisation". A Framework of Analysis*, in *The International Lawyer*, 2001, 1589.

centre, we now move on to the quest for the third factor usually found in political regimes, and that is legitimacy".[72]

The fact that globalisation is a phenomenon connected to the crisis in law and, more in general, to the crisis in sovereignty, has also been noted by F. Galgano: "This decline is more generally associated with the crisis in State sovereignty, of which Natalino Irti spoke [...] as a 'tattered shred'. On this point there is now an interdisciplinary convergence of views: Sabino Cassese spoke of the State's 'retreat' from its classic functions; [...] Maria Rosa Ferrarese uses the term 'dimming' of sovereignty".[73]

Globalisation and integration have been spoken of as the result of a process of "purification" in philosophical reasoning at the end of the 19th and in the first decades of the 20th centuries, but also and to an equal extent, on a historical level, as new concepts reborn, like the mythical phoenix, out of the ashes of two world conflicts.

The requirement to establish new economic relationships is undoubtedly symptomatic of such a desire for rebirth of the individual States, which gradually begin to admit the need to surrender part of their sovereignty and to cooperate fairly in order to build a system that guarantees trade flow and transparent information. There is therefore a tight link between the trend towards globalisation and a market directed economy: "with the advent of the global market, the economy becomes disassociated from politics. [...] The current decline in public governance of the economy is not, on closer examination, only the consequence of a conversion towards liberalism. [...] The relationship between State and market has been reversed: now the market [...] is the source that assesses the public securities issued by the States and that influences their financial policy".[74]

Here again Weber' notion emerges that there exists a possibility for economic phenomena to become a vehicle for the dissemination of legal approaches, of a leading role of the economy in the way law evolves.

72 S. Cassese, *Lo spazio giuridico globale cit.*, 10: "Esclusa l'esistenza di un'autorità superiore, da cui dipende una gerarchia di apparati, ma riconosciuta, invece, la presenza di tutti gli elementi di un ordinamento giuridico internazionale, ammesso che quest'ultimo presenta un'organizzazione complessa, senza, tuttavia un centro, si passa ora, alla ricerca del terzo fattore solitamente presente nei regimi politici, che è quello della legittimazione". See also V. Schmidt, *Democracy and Europe in an integrating Europe and a Globalising World*, in *European Law Journal*, vol. 6, n. 3, 2000, 277 "the public has to be convinced by the government and related policy elites that the choice is not just necessary but also appropriate. This is facilitated by the construction of a discourse that projects a coherent vision of how the nations fits into an integrating Europe and a globalising world that also taps into deeper structure of national values and identity".

73 F. Galgano, *La globalizzazione e le fonti del diritto*, in *Riv. trim. dir. pubbl.*, 2, 2006, 215: "Questo declino si lega più in generale alla crisi della sovranità dello Stato, della quale Natalino Irti ha parlato [...] come di un 'lacero brandello'. Sul punto c'è ormai una interdisciplinare convergenza di vedute: Sabino Cassese ha parlato di 'arretramento' dello Stato dalle sue classiche funzioni; [...] Maria Rosaria Ferrarese si è espressa in termini di 'appannamento' della sovranità".

74 F. Galgano, *La globalizzazione e le fonti del diritto cit.*, 315: "Con l'avvento del mercato globale l'economia si dissocia dalla politica. [...] L'odierno declino del governo pubblico dell'economia non è, a ben vedere, solo il portato di una conversione al liberalismo. [...] Il rapporto tra Stato e mercato si è invertito: è il mercato [...] la fonte che giudica i titoli del debito pubblico emessi dagli Stati e che condiziona la politica finanziaria di questi ultimi".

As regards globalisation, economic in the first place and then legal, a second trend was identified, that of the enhancing of national profiles, that creates a counter-thrust in opposition to the tendencies of globalisation and integration.[75] These two tendencies if not appropriately managed, may lead to a breakdown in the system. The remedy to a similar kind of ill must be found in the development of a principle that may reconcile these two impulses. It was probably with this purpose in mind that Article 5 (3b) of the Treaty was drawn up, expounding the principle of subsidiarity.[76]

In concluding this introductory chapter, it seems therefore appropriate to retrace the essential features of a principle which is so important in the discipline of Community dynamics.

7. The adhesive between globalisation and autonomistic tendencies: the principle of subsidiarity

The principle of subsidiarity is at the heart of the apportionment of the competencies between the Union and Member States in the procedure of forming popular will.[77]

[75] C. Pinelli, *Cittadini, responsabilità politica, mercati globali*, in AA.VV., *Studi in onore di Leopoldo Elia*, vol. II, Milano, 1000, 1257. On globalised standards in financial systems, see M. De Bellis, *Gli* standards *globali per i servizi finanziari: concorrenza e reciproco rafforzamento tra diversi modelli di amministrazione globale* in S. Cassese, M. Conticelli, *Diritto e amministrazioni nello spazio giuridico globale*, in *Quaderni della Rivista trimestrale di diritto pubblico*, Milano, 2006, 154.

[76] L. Oliveri, *Sovranità popolare, sovranità e statualità tra Carta Europea dei Diritti dell'Uomo e "Futuro dell'Europa"*, in *Riv. it. dir. pubbl. com.*, 2004, 33.

[77] A. D'Atena, *Modelli federali e sussidiarietà nel riparto delle competenze normative tra l'Unione europea e gli Stati membri*, in *Diritto dell'Unione Europea*, 2005, 51; ID. *Sussidiarietà e sovranità*, in AA.VV., *Sopranazionalità europea: posizioni soggettive e normazione*, n. 7, *Quaderni del Consiglio di Stato*, Torino, 2000, 178; ID., *Constitutión y principio de subsidiariedad*, in *Repertorio Aranzadi del Tribunal Constitucional*, n. 12/2001, 5; ID., *Subsidiarity and Division of Competencies between European Union, its Member States and their Regions*, in I. Pernice – R. Miccù (eds.), *The European Constitution in the Making*, Baden Baden, 2003, 144. G. Strozzi, *Il principio di sussidiarietà nel Trattato di Maastricht*, in *Rivista di diritto internazionale*, 1992, 376 ff.; H. Bribosia, *Subsidiarité et répartition des competences entre la Communauté et ses Etats membres. Commentaire sur l'article 3B du Traité de Maastricht*, in *Revue du Marché Unique Européen*, 1992, 165 ff.; A.G. Toth, *The principle of Subsidiarity in the Maastricht Treaty*, in *Common Market Law Review*, 1992, 1079 ff.; L. Vandelli, *Il principio di sussidiarietà nel riparto di competenze tra diversi livelli territoriali: a proposito dell'art. 3 B del Trattato sull'Unione Europea*, in *Riv.it. di dir. pubbl. com.*, 1993, 379 ff.; K. Lenaerts – P. Van Yoersele, *Le principe de subsidiarité et son contexte: étude de l'article 3 B du Traité CE*, in *Cahiers du droit européen*, 1994, 86 ff.; E. Vinci, *Sussidiarietà, democrazia e trasparenza nel Trattato di Maastricht*, in *Jus*, 1994, 353 ff.; V. Harrison, *Subsidiarity in Article 3b of the EC Treaty: gobbledegook or justiciable principle?*, in *International and Compartive Law Quarterly*, 1996, 431 ff.; G. Majone, *"Democracy Deficit": The Question of Standards*, *European Law Journal* 1997, 5; ID., M. Everson, *Institutional reform: independent agencies, oversight, coordination and procedural control*, in O. De Schutter, N. Lebessis, J. Paterson (ed.), *Governance in the European Union*, Luxembourg, 1997, 129; F. Mayer, *Kompetenzüberschreitung und Letztentscheidung. Das Masstricht-Urteil des Bundesverfassungsgerichts und die Letztentscheidung über Ultra vires-Akte in Mehrebenensystemen*, München, 2000; cfr. A.F. Utz, *Die geistesgeschichtlichen Grundlagen des Subsidiaritätsprinzip*, in *Der Subsidiaritätsprinzip*, herausgegeben von A.F. Utz, Heidelberg 1953, 7 ff., spec. 13 ff.; J. Höffner, *Christliche Gesellschaftslehre, 8. erweiterte Auflage*, *Kevelaer* 1983, trad. it. di C. Danna, *La dottrina sociale cristiana*, Cinisello Balsamo 1987, 42; O. Von

As already mentioned, the principle was introduced by the Treaty of Maastricht, accepted by Community law and then taken up again in the European Constitution signed in Rome on 29 September 2004.

The European Constitution also contained explicit recognition of the supervisory role carried out by national parliaments, in accordance with the provisions of the protocol attached to the treaty.

In particular, the protocol provides for the immediate reporting to the national Parliaments of the legislative proposals of the Commission, the legislative resolutions of the European Parliament and the positions of the Council. It also specifies that each national parliament, or both the chambers they consist of, have the faculty of conveying expert opinions to the European Parliament, the Council and the Commission, on abuses of the principle of subsidiarity; the Commission is also charged with a duty of review.

A similar function to that of the national parliaments was awarded to the Committee of the Regions, to which the power of appeal to the Court of Justice was given, to report any violation of the principle of subsidiarity, in cases where such violation is due to legislative acts on which its consultation is required.

Indisputably, aside from the contingent outcomes of the European Constitution, recognition of the importance of the national Parliaments demonstrates the specific will to implement so-called "*bottom up subsidiarity*", by means of a "policy of ends" of Kantian inspiration, not centralised nor hierarchical, but organised as interaction on many levels, regional, national and supranational.

The idea of participation "from below" in the formation of the normative framework, combining the typical characteristics of both the reticular model and Habermas's model (in its dual non-hierarchic and participatory nature) is united with the need for a "disclosure philosophy" that constitutes the cornerstone of the regulatory system set up by the individual national systems in defence of the transparency of market operations.

Now it is necessary to investigate how this model applies in the system of independent authorities, in particular, in those authorities assigned to the supervision of financial markets. It has been observed, in this regard: "The markets [...] meet with various kinds of 'failure'; these include the formation of monopolies and natural oligopolies, the creation of income from excessive dominant position [...]. In the scenarios mentioned above, the market, if left completely 'free' would end up re-acquiring the traits of a monopolistic market and inevitably would reproduce the same disadvantages. [...] The fundamental function of the regulatory authorities is, precisely, to avoid the occurrence of such events, that would jeopardise the efficiency and equilibrium of the economic system and would nullify the benefits of privatisation[78]".

Nell-Breuning, *Baugesetze der Gesellschaft, Solidarität und Subsidiarität*, Freiburg i. Br. 1990, 87 ff.; C. Millon- Delsol, *Le principe de subsidiarité*, Paris 1993, 12 ff.

78 F. Gaffuri, *Governo e autorità di regolazione nel servizio energetico*, in *Diritto Amministrativo*, 1999, 2, 331: "I mercati [...] incorrono in diversi tipi di 'fallimenti'; in questi rientrano la Formazione di monopoli ed oligopoli naturali, la creazione di rendite di posizione eccessiva [...]. Nelle ipotesi sopramenzionate, il mercato, lasciato del tutto 'libero' finirebbe per riacquisire, in sostanza, i connotati di un mercato monopolistico e inevitabilmente riproporrebbe gli stessi inconvenienti. [...] Funzione fondamentale delle autorità di regolazione è, per l'appunto, quella di evitare il verificarsi di simili

The irrefutable presence in the market of purely speculative phenomena and the attested low reliability of a system based on spontaneous reporting confirm the need, in this sector, for a system of uniform and transparent rules.

This point will be further explored below. However, first we will try to complete the picture, by examining the same topics, previously seen from a theoretical perspective, from the angle of the scholars of financial economics.

evenienze, che pregiudicherebbero l'efficienza e l'equilibrio del sistema economico e annullerebbero i benefici della privatizzazione".

Chapter 2

CHAPTER 2. THE ECONOMIC SUBSTRATUM

1. Introduction: the supervisory authorities in the financial system, between economic principles and global standards

From a theoretical viewpoint, independent authorities operate within a context of progressive modification of the notion of sovereignty, in the sense of national sovereignty that, from being a mere privilege of the single states, takes on a "transversal" nature. From an economic viewpoint, appointing independent authorities for supervision of the market seem to be necessary in order to guarantee, given the complexity of market relations, an adequate degree of security and transparency.

The close connection between economic and legal models has been examined, and Weber's teachings still apply, according to which an economic structure is essential for the promotion of legal frameworks.

Nevertheless warnings made by Habermas, continuing on from Weber, should not be forgotten. He urges us to consider the economy as a realm in which democratic ideals may be fully achieved, on the strength of the very nature of the market-directed economy, the cradle of free trade and of the emergence and consolidation of agreements between the actors that operate in it.

Moreover, when speaking of the economy, we are conditioned to qualify it as "global".

For these reasons, a brief overview of key economic notions is now necessary; we will also look at the actors that, in a global law scenario, deal on various levels with the problem of supervision of market operations (most importantly the European Central Bank). There will be a focus on the proposals put forward to "nourish" the system and encourage its development (we will refer to the Lamfalussy Committee and to the two Basel Committees). Lastly we will look at the main Community sources of law, that, in the frenetic endeavour to implement global standards, constitute the connective tissue of legal rules to be applied in the single Member States. Analysis of Directives is organised in two sections: the first is entirely about provisions concerning transparency (pillar III); the last section addresses the realisation of the 1st and 2nd pillars (minimum capital requirements and prudential control). The reason for dividing Community legal sources into these two sections is dictated by one circumstance of a temporal nature and one of a logical nature: regulations on transparency were implemented before all the others and they constitute a distinct *corpus* compared to the content of the first and second pillars, that are quite closely connected to the extent that they are often disciplined together on a Community level.

In short, the following observation is relevant: "the study of parsimony stands at the crossroads between economic and legal science: the former is essential for what could be defined as the structure of the savings system, that is all the models and instruments for use of available resources [...], the latter cannot avoid asking questions as to the group of rules that define the conditions in which the savings-production circuit works, rules which have been becoming ever more complex and sophisticated".[79]

2. Introductory outline of the financial system

The financial system may be defined as the organised combination of financial markets, intermediaries and instruments, the structure through which, in a modern economy, financial activity is conducted. It also includes, through the production and supply of financial services, the three fundamental processes of the functioning of the economy: the regulation of trade, the accumulation of savings and financing of investments, and risk management.[80]

More specifically, the financial market is formed by the bodies, instruments and technology that facilitate the transfer of financial means from the operators and sectors who have a financial surplus to the operators and sectors who instead show a financial deficit; in other words they spend more than their earnings on consumption, investment or on goods.

Because the meeting between suppliers and seekers of funds is not always easy, due to the differences in the needs of the two parties, the relations which are established between them are almost exclusively aimed at the issue of securities on the financial market: securities are the financial instrument forming the relationship between the two parties.

The securities market thus becomes an arena in which all financial operations are performed that involve securities, that is financial instruments which are able to move

[79] S. Dettori, A. Zito, *Risparmio (tutela del)*, in *Trattato di diritto amministrativo europeo*, M.P. Chiti and G. Greco, (eds.) G.F. Cartei and D.U. Galetta, Parte speciale, Tomo III, II ed., Milano, 2007, 1732: "Lo studio del risparmio si pone al crocevia tra scienza economica e scienza giuridica: se dalla prima non si può prescindere per quella che potrebbe definirsi la struttura del sistema del risparmio, ossia l'insieme dei modelli e degli strumenti di impiego delle risorse disponibili [...], la seconda non può fare a meno di interrogarsi sull'insieme di regole che definiscono le condizioni attraverso le quali si dipana il circuito risparmio-produzione, regole che si sono fatte sempre più complesse e sofisticate". See also G. Montedoro, *Le amministrazioni indipendenti e la vigilanza sui mercati finanziari*, in *Foro amm. CdS*, 2004, 10, 2998.

[80] G. Forestieri, P. Mottura, *Il sistema finanziario. Istituzioni, mercati e modelli di intermediazione*, Milano, II ed., 2000; A. Ferrari, F. Gualandri, A. Landi, P. Vezzani, *Strumenti, mercati, intermediari finanziari*, Torino, 1997; G. Ferrari, P. Marchetti (eds.), *La riforma dei mercati finanziari*, Milano, 1998. See also J.H. Dalhuisen, *Financial Services, Products, Risks and Regulation in Europe after the EU 1998 Action Plan and Basle II*, in *EBLR*, 819, 2007.

easily between operators, because they are provided with a high degree of mobility and transferability.

Thus financial markets tend to be differentiated and segmented according to various factors, among which the following are included:

a) category of financial instruments negotiated, leading to the differentiation between the monetary market (short term instruments), the capital market (stocks and bonds) and derivatives markets (futures, options);
b) geographic dimension (national, international);
c) institutional nature (regulated markets and non-regulated markets; public or private);
d) logistic structure (physical markets, telematics markets);
e) negotiation procedures (public auction, *market making*).

The main function of the intermediaries operating on the financial market consists in facilitating the issue and subsequent negotiation of financial instruments.

This means that they operate both in the area of the market where financial instruments are issued (the primary market) and in the area where their subsequent negotiation takes place (the secondary market). Generally intermediaries are enterprises specialised in the production of financial instruments, in their negotiation, and in providing consultancy services connected with the above activities.

As an extreme oversimplification, these intermediaries may be classified into a few main categories:

a) Credit intermediaries, characterised by their credit function, on the assets side, and by so-called "nominalistic" liability (obligation to repay at nominal value); banks are a special category of credit intermediaries, distinguished by their performance of a monetary function;
b) Financial intermediaries, which are mainly active in negotiation, administration and consultancy in relation to financial instruments;
c) Insurance companies, distinguished by their risk management function and by a collateral financial circuit, structured as follows: premiums, reserves investments, payment of insured capital.

A further distinction that analysts and experts in financial science usually make is the distinction between the "institutional" perspective, as it were, and the "functional" perspective. This relates to how the phenomenon of intermediation is seen: the former is based on institutional categories, and the latter on the economic functions carried out, on how they are combined and, therefore, on the functions of the intermediaries.

3. Control of the financial system: objectives

The objectives of control of the financial system consist in the two large areas of the objectives of monetary policy and the objectives of regulation and supervision: the former are part of a more general side of economic policy, while the latter aim for the stability and efficiency of the financial system.

Stability relates to savers' need for protection and the functionality of the payment system; efficiency may be understood in the dual sense of operative efficiency, meaning the cost of financial activity to the real economy, and allocative efficiency, meaning the level of quality of the process of implementation of available resources.

Here we find justification for the need to set up an efficient system of regulation that is situated in a dimension of dynamic, almost contrapuntal, dialogue with market forces, on one hand keeping down the level of competition for the businesses that threaten to alter the processes of distribution of income and allocation of resources (and implementing so-called *"economic regulation"*), and on the other hand protecting the safety of the consumers of goods and services in all the cases where direct control is excessively burdensome or even impossible (so-called *"social regulation"*).

Therefore it is clear that regulation is the keystone to the "forte crise de confiance"[81] that has struck the world economy: "c'est la régulation qui est aujourd'hui le maître-mot pour trouver une solution à toute désordre économique ou financier".[82]

The reasons underlying the choice of a particular order in the financial market may vary, depending on if one supports a "positive" vision of the phenomena of special regulation of economic activity, considering them as remedies to market failures, or, on the contrary, if one is convinced by the more cynical view of this phenomenon, according to which every form of regulation constitutes "a method to extract profit on the part of different pressure groups (companies active in the regulated sector of the economy, politicians, officials of the supervisory authorities etc), on whose wellbeing regulation may have consequences (theory of public choice)".[83]

81 J.F. Lepetit, *Entretien de la COB 2002, Bull. COB*, n. 373, 2002, 3.

82 J.P. Valette, *La régulation des marchés financiers, in Revue du droit public,* 2005, 184: "Sa référence fait parfois craindre un concept mystérieux, fourre-tout et catalogué, mais elle s'impose chaque jour davantage. La régulation a été définié récemment par le Conseil économique et social français comme l'exercice d'une relation pacifiée entre les acteurs économiques, s'appuyant sur une autorité reconnue, permettant de surmonter les conflits d'intérêts. En matière économique et financière, elle peut se réduire à trois paramètres: une intervention fondamentalement publique (mais indépendante du gouvernement), une action sur un ou plusieurs marchés, la création d'un cadre loyal et sécurisé de concurrence". Id., *Le service public à la française*, Ellipses, 2000, 158.

83 R. Costi – L. Enriques, *Il mercato mobiliare*, in *Trattato di diritto commerciale*, dir. da G. Cottino, vol. VIII, Padova, 2004, 7: *"un mezzo per estrarre rendite da parte dei diversi gruppi di interesse (imprese attive nel settore economico regolato, politici, funzionari delle autorità di vigilanza ecc.), sul cui benessere la regolamentazione può incidere (teoria delle scelte pubbliche)"*; T. Padoa Schioppa, *Sistema finanziario e regolamentazione, in Bollettino Economico della Banca d'Italia*, n. 11, 1988; R. Caparvi (cur.by) *Il mercato mobiliare italiano. Strutture e tendenze evolutive*, Milano, 2003; R. Costi, *L'ordinamento bancario*, Bologna, 2001, 201; Benston, *Consumer Protection as Justification for Regulating Financial-Services and Products*, in *Journal of Financial Services Research*, 2000, 277, 282; P.A. Cucurachi, *I profili organizzativi dei sistemi di vigilanza bancaria*, Milano, 1997; Ferrarini – Marchetti (ed.), *La riforma dei mercati finanziari dal decreto Eurosim al Testo Unico della finanza*, Roma, 1998.

Support of one or the other theory does not constitute an obstacle to the recognition of common ground between the two, drawing on the same need to preserve the stability and efficiency of the securities market.

More specifically, the theoretical premises underlying the regulation of the financial system may be summed up in the need to protect the consumers of financial services, to control credit and monetary aggregates and related prices, and, finally, to define the optimum competition structure.[84]

The need for consumer protection is demonstrated by the occurrence of a series of *market failures*, the most important being the bearing of transaction costs, the existence of information imbalances and related agency costs, and the limited rationality of operators. These factors constitute the main reasons for the creation of financial intermediaries and for their regulation.

In parallel to this first need, which may be ascribed to the model of social regulation, the need arises to guarantee that the financial system operates in conditions of efficiency, that can be achieved through the introduction of constraints on the activities of the intermediaries, in order to ensure an effective supervision of monetary and credit institutions.

The third aspect of economic regulation can be seen in the need to define the optimum competition framework for the financial system, which aims to limit market power and to reduce the level of competition.

It emerges, from what has been said so far, that the complex system of public intervention in economics may have at least two aspects, one related to monetary policy and the other to supervision policy. The latter is gaining increasing importance as financial systems evolve, in a context of progressive integration at both international and Community level.

4. From the notion of market to that of "financial conglomerate"

Examination of questions connected to supervision entails a further methodological premise, in order to draw Cartesian coordinates within which to place the activities and the functions of the authorities supervising the financial sector.

In particular, while studying the work of the authorities mentioned above, it is possible to apply different levels of reading, as with orchestral scores: a first "spatial" level of reading, as it were, is connected with the authorities' "topographic" placement. This could be viewed from a more conceptual perspective, tracing back the functions of independent administrations to the monitoring of market transparency, as the principle underlying the banking, credit and insurance sectors.

First and foremost it must be noted how the notion of financial market, together with the demarcation of the boundaries within which supervision must be carried out, has

84 Llewellin, *The Economic Rationale for Financial Regulation*, *FSA Occasional Paper*, n. 1, 1999, 22; Spencer, *The Structure and Regulation of Financial Markets*, Oxford, 2000, 34; Pacces, *Financial Intermediation in the Securities Markets: Law and Economics of Conduct of Business Regulation*, in *International Review of Law and Economics*, 2000, 479.

experienced progressive downsizing, followed by a more precise definition of the sectors within which the independent bodies are obliged to operate.

Research on regulation of the financial system requires, therefore, prior reflection on the concept of the regulated market, understood as the location where the supply of investors' financial resources meets the demand of companies for finance.[85]

In order to illustrate this point, it is possible to distinguish, among the most widespread market models, three different typologies: the so-called direct market in which the contracting parties directly negotiate the conditions which regulate capital trade; the open market where negotiation is carried out through the use of standardised instruments and according to predetermined rules and conditions; and finally the foreign exchange market, which is formed by all the foreign currency negotiations that banks and other financial operators constantly exchange.

In turn, within the concept of open market, a distinction can be made between the monetary market, which comprises all short-term negotiations for capital, and the financial market which includes middle and long term negotiations for capital.

The convergence of supply and demand between actors operating in the financial system is facilitated by the intermediaries: these include banking intermediaries, or banks, whose main activity consists in gathering "deposits or other repayable funds" from the public; and non-banking intermediaries (insurance companies and welfare institutions, leasing and factoring firms, companies who manage common investment funds, businesses acting as securities intermediaries, and merchant banks).

Community legislation has contributed significantly to the regulation of finance. In particular, Directive n. 93/22 CEE of 10 May 1993[86], concerning investment services in the securities sector, established guidelines required to define the typologies of regulated markets and the prerequisites needed to ensure its correct functioning.

As studies have shown, the phrase "regulated markets", adopted in Directive n. 93/22, is not new to Community law on securities intermediation. It was first used in Directive n. 79/279 of 5 March 1979 on the topic of admission to stock-exchange listing; it was subsequently adopted by Directive n. 89/952 of 13 November 1989, on insider trading, with the aim of defining its area of application.[87]

Moreover, in the detail of the directives on financial matters, it is possible to trace the objectives that Community law seeks to pursue. For example it is useful to recall the provisions of Directive n. 2002/87/CE of the European Parliament and of the Council of 16 December 2002, explicitly recognising the need to develop adequate forms of supervision over financial conglomerates.

85 A. Segni, *I mercati e i valori mobiliari*, 2187, in Cassese (ed.), *Diritto amministrativo speciale*, III, *Finanza pubblica e privata. La disciplina dell'economia*, Milano, 2003.

86 *OJ 11 June* 1993, n. 141/27.

87 F. Amtenbrink, *The Democratic Accountability of Central Banks. A Comparative Study of the European Central Bank*, Oxford and Portland, Oregon, 1999; A. Brozzetti, V. Santoro, *Le direttive comunitarie in materia bancaria e l'ordinamento italiano*, Milano, 1990; L. Costi, *Mercati finanziari*, Torino 2000; C. Conti, *La disciplina del mercato mobiliare: dal diritto della borsa al testo unico della Finanza*, Padova, 2001.

An indispensable precondition to ensuring such control is definition of the boundaries within which the supervisory authorities must operate.

With this view of circumscribing with greater care the system of controls, the notion of "regulated market" is associated with that of "financial conglomerate": "To be effective, further supervision of credit institutions, of insurance companies and of investment firms belonging to a financial conglomerate should be carried out on all such conglomerates with significant inter-sectorial financial activities".

In Article 4 the criteria used to identify a financial conglomerate are listed, confirming the trend towards a system that is no longer organised in terms of market supervision intended in the broad sense but rather on specific and distinct sectors of the market, consisting of groups of credit organisations, insurance companies and investment companies, that are part of a financial conglomerate.

At this point it is worth pointing out the clear shift towards a system in which authorities cooperate and coordinate with each other in a much more uniform fashion compared to the past.

Regarding this point it is useful to mention the content of Article 27, modifying the text of Directive n. 93/22: "the relevant competent authorities [...] shall in particular consult each other when assessing the suitability of the shareholders and the reputation and experience of directors involved in the management of another entity of the same group. They shall inform each other of any information regarding the suitability of shareholders and the reputation and experience of directors which is of relevance to the other competent authorities involved, for the granting of an authorisation as well as for the ongoing assessment of compliance with operating conditions".

The introduction of supplementary supervision constitutes therefore the first stage of the plan of action formulated by the European Commission to ensure strengthened supervision over financial groups belonging to a financial conglomerate.

Subsequent steps towards a system which is increasingly oriented towards the promotion of exchange and co-ordination between supervisory authorities are seen in two decisions made by the Commission on 5 November 2003, which founded the Committee of European Banking Supervisors (CEBS) and the European Banking Committee (EBC).

The unifying element of the two provisions lies precisely in the reference to the same field for action where both the European Banking Committee and the Committee of European Banking Supervisors are required to operate, co-ordinating with each other in monitoring the activities of different financial conglomerates.

5. Models of supervision

Before proceeding to look at the main models of supervision in operation today, it will be necessary to identify, although very broadly, the guidelines to be followed in clarifying the distinguishing criteria of these models.

As regards types of supervision, four different functions can be identified, each one connected with one or more methods of action, concerning in particular:

1) formulation of rules that imply specific prohibitions or duties applicable to homogeneous categories of intermediaries.
2) forecasting of objective requirements, compliance with which implies acquisition of the right to be granted the authorisations necessary to perform certain activities of financial intermediation;
3) granting of authorisations on a discretional basis;
4) systematic recourse to forms of moral suasion, made necessary by the non-attribution of specific powers.

In addition, by crossing supervision styles with supervisory instruments it is possible to identify two separate models of regulation.

The first, related to the *referee model*, is distinguished by a moderate degree of discretionary power and by recourse to forms of control based on capital coefficients and on transparent and objective rules of conduct.

The second, the *director model*, is mainly aimed at the use of instruments of an administrative nature: the organisational model can be observed both on a macro-structural and on a micro-structural level of supervision.

The first case refers to the allocation of control responsibilities and the political choices related to the decision to establish new authorities in the form of government agencies, of autonomous public bodies, or of self-regulating organisations. In the second case, appraisal is made of the internal organisational structure of each single authority, with the objective of verifying the attainment of the objectives assigned to them.

Supervision activity may follow one of two alternative models: a "centralised" model, in which there is only one authority that regulates and controls all the sections of the financial market, both the products and the intermediaries, as well as the various aims of supervision; a "decentralised" model, in which supervisors are defined according to the competencies they have been assigned, and divided into supervision for institutions, functional supervision and supervision by objectives.[88]

Put very simply, of the models existent in Europe, one model provides for a single supervisory authority, responsible for carrying out "transversal" supervisory activity on the market, and the other provides for the establishment of one authority for every market sector which needs to be controlled. We do not want to indulge in generalisations and run the risk of reducing the problems pertaining to the choice of supervisory model

88 K. Lannoo, *Supervising the European Financial System*, in P. Cecchini, F. Heinemann, M. Jopp (eds.), *The Incomplete European Market for Financial Services*, Heidelberg, 2003, 232: "the exercise of banking supervision under the roof of the central bank was seen a barrier towards a more overall integrated supervision of financial sector as a whole [...]. Norway integrated bank and insurance supervision in 1986, followed by Denmark in 1988 and Sweden in 1992. The most exemplified, however, was the creation of the UK Financial Services Authority (FSA) in May 1997, which regrouped 7 different financial sector supervisory authority. The German FSA, the Federal Agency for Financial Market Supervision, was proposed in January 2001 and formally started in May 2002, although some important exceptions remain, such as leaving the supervision of securities markets in the hands of the *Länder*. Moreover, the German structure will remain decentralised for some time to come, which raises question about its operational effectiveness. The FSA in Austria started to function in April 2002. In Belgium and Ireland, financial supervision will be integrated under the aegis of the central bank".

to a rigid separation between the single integrated model and the pluralistic model where different authorities cover the sectors to be supervised; but it is easy to share the opinion of those who tend to support a model of supervision centred on the diversification of its functions, rather than a single "Leviathan" authority, which may be reassuring for the whole financial market[89], but is also rather paralysing for potential investments: "one possible model calls for one agency to carry out surveillance separately for systemic stability reasons, a second for prudential motives and a third for conduct-of-business".[90]

The choice of which model of supervision of financial institutions to adopt does not only relate, in reality, to identification of the sectors which authorities are assigned to supervise, but is also connected to the possibility of concentrating supervisory activity on a single subject.

As will be seen in more depth below, in the key countries of the European Union, the process of concentration in the banking sector has been gradually diversifying through the creation of heterogeneous financial conglomerates. In this context, legal and political debate has concentrated on whether it was better to maintain the traditional structure, that provides for the existence of various authorities, or rather to combine all supervisory activity under a single organism, responsible for pursuing the aims of transparency, stability and protection of investors in all sectors of the financial markets.[91]

6. The "centralised" model of supervision

In the centralised model there exists a sole authority, that regulates and controls all segments of the financial market, both as regards types of products and of intermediaries, and as regards the different purposes of supervision. Fundamentally, control of all markets and intermediaries is assigned to a single regulator, regardless of their nature, be it banking, securities or insurance, and of the diverse purposes of regulation.

As will be seen below, this model has found concrete application in the UK legal system, through the establishment of the *Financial Services Authority*, as well as in the German and Austrian legal systems.

[89] K. Lannoo, *Supervising the European Financial System cit.*, 234: "a Leviatan supervisor could create the perception that the whole financial sector is secure. It may reduce the incentives for providers to prudently manage their business, and for users to carefully choose their financial services' provider, the so called moral hazard".

[90] K. Lannoo, *Supervising the European Financial System cit.*, 231: "it has been argued that the crucial thing is not whether all the functional supervisors are under a single roof, but whether they communicate with one another. This is not a simple task, if one images that the British FSA employs about 2000 persons. If an integrated supervisor is no more than a combination of banking, insurance and investment business divisions, the full benefits of a single regulatory authority will not be achieved".

[91] M. Quagliariello, *L'assetto istituzionale della vigilanza finanziaria: il dibattito in letteratura*, disponibile sul sito della BCE www.ecb.int; T. Padoa Schioppa, *Securities and banking: bridges and walls, Lecture at the London School of Economics, London*, 21 January 2002, in www.ecb.int. *See also* C. Gerster – G. Klein – H. Schoppmann – D. Schwander – C. Wengler, *European Banking and Financial Services Law*, Kluwer Law International, 2004; and M. Megliani, *Il quadro evolutivo dei mercati finanziari europei nella prospettiva internazionale*, in *Banca borsa tit. credito*, 2004, 677.

According to the promoters of the centralised model, it offers the advantage of greater effectiveness and unity in supervision: centralisation of the functions of supervision into a single body allows the system, at the same time, to achieve scale economies, by reducing the administrative costs and responsibilities for the operators.

The concentration of the different objectives of supervision in a single body constitutes a risk for inefficiency, since the correct working of the single regulator depends largely on its internal organisation.[92]

Consequently, since forms of supervision where division of responsibilities is decided according to type of subject supervised and to type of service provided to the subject seem to run the risk of creating excessive lack of homogeneity in regulation, with consequent fragmentation of control over supervised subjects[93], the Italian parliament opted for the model of supervision by purpose, as apparently the most suited to regulating the financial market.[94]

7. The "decentralised" model of supervision

In the decentralised model, a number of regulators exist, so that the allocation of responsibilities may be carried out in relation to the typology of the subjects supervised (supervision by institution), the purposes of the invigilation (supervision by purpose) and the type of service supplied (supervision by activity).

The first type is characterised by the fact that supervision is carried out on all categories of financial operators: typical of this approach is the presence within each system of at least three distinct supervisory and regulatory authorities: for banks, for financial intermediaries and for insurance companies, in other words for each of the corresponding market segments. The criticism which is made most often regarding the pure institutional model is that, although it results in an irrefutable simplification of the organisational structure and a reduction of the costs of supervision, it does not appear to be wholly suited to meeting "the growing tendency towards the de-specialization of intermediaries, and the increasing integration of markets and similarities in typologies of financial instruments".[95]

92 G. Sabatini, *La vigilanza sugli intermediari e sui mercati*, in A. Banfi (ed.), *I mercati e gli strumenti finanziari. Disciplina e organizzazione della borsa*, Torino, 2004, 251.

93 J.H. Dalhuisen, *Financial services, products, risks and regulation*, in *EBLR cit.*, 839; C. Goodhart et al., *Financial Regulation: Why, How and Where Now?, London Routleged, 1998;* and C. Ford and J. Kay, *Why Regulate Financial Markets*, in F. Oditah (ed.), *The Future for the Global Securities Market*, Oxford, OUP, 1996.

94 M.C. Quirici, *Il sistema di vigilanza sugli intermediari*, in R. Caparvi (ed.), *Il nuovo mercato mobiliare italiano cit.*, 213; A.P. Soda, *I nuovi criteri di vigilanza sugli intermediari e sui mercati in relazione alla direttiva sui servizi di investimento*, in *Rivista bancaria*, 6, 1995, 138; A.N. Licht, *Stock Exchange Mobility, Unilateral Recognition, and the Privatization of Securities Regulation*, in *Virginia Journal of International Law*, 2001, in part. 607.

95 G. Sabatini, *La vigilanza sugli intermediari e sui mercati cit.*, 454: "la progressiva tendenza alla despecializzazione degli intermediari e alla crescente integrazione dei mercati e assimilazione delle tipologie degli strumenti finanziari". In this regard G. Forestieri, P. Mottura, *Il sistema finanziario*,

The model of supervision by purpose consists in subjecting intermediaries, or markets, to control by a number of authorities, each appointed to pursue one of the regulatory objectives, regardless of the legal form of the intermediaries and of the activities performed by them.

Such a structure produces the advantage of enabling effective control and homogeneous regulation of subjects that, although they have diverse legal forms, carry out the same activity within a context of strongly integrated markets, in which multifunctional intermediaries and multi-sector groups operate.

On the other hand, this model, because of the existence of various authorities, involves the risk of a not insignificant increase in supervision costs for operators; they may face duplicate controls, since they are obliged to transmit to each authority appropriate supervision reports containing information which is often identical or very similar.[96]

Finally, the model of supervision by activity is structured in such a manner that a special supervisory authority corresponds to each category of financial intermediation, so that, in a similar way to the model by purpose, there is the advantage of uniform rules for subjects which carry out the same activity, even if they are bound by different legal structures and forms.

However, even in this model, similarly to the model of supervision by purpose, there still seems to be no solution to the problem of the risks that the conflict between different supervision purposes, pursued by the same authority, reduces the efficiency and effectiveness of action.

Finally, the model of organising supervision and regulation responsibilities based on "functions" needs to be briefly mentioned. In practice this model has been usually used to justify the organisation of supervisory functions with regard to the nature of the activities performed by the intermediaries (banking, securities and insurance). In this way, the model under examination has ended up by resembling the activity model, based on the consideration that each type of financial intermediation activity corresponds to the economic functions of the financial system.[97]

8. Coordination between supervisory models. The case of the European Central Bank

The process leading to the identification of supervision models at Community level developed in parallel to the establishment of independent European regulatory authorities, such as the European System of Central Banks (ESCB) and the European Central Bank (ECB), the European Mediator, the European Data Protection Supervisor (EDPS) and the European Food Safety Authority (EFSA).

Milano, 2002; F. Di Pasquali, *La disciplina dell'intermediazione e dei mercati finanziari*, Milano, 2001; A. Banfi, *Tecnica dei valori mobiliari*, Torino, 2002.

96 G. Sabatini, *La vigilanza sugli intermediari cit.*, 455; N. Salanitro, *Società per azioni e mercati finanziari*, Milano, 1999.

97 M. Anolli, *Elementi di economia del mercato mobiliare*, 2001, Bologna; C. Vaciago, G. Verga, *Efficienza e stabilità dei mercati finanziari*, Bologna, 1995.

These authorities do not present characteristics which are essentially different from the organisations established within the member States. But, from another point of view, they contribute to the reconciling, moderating and regulating of different needs, ensuring, in ultimate analysis, their equilibrium.[98]

A good example in the banking and credit system is the European Central Bank, that has the primary responsibility of ensuring the implementation of monetary policy objectives given in the Treaty founding the European Community.[99]

Two brief points must be made regarding the legal nature of the Central Bank and its powers in the area of prudential supervision.

To begin with, the issue concerning its legal nature has been the object of extensive debate: it is sometimes qualified as a "quasi-institution", or as a "Community body", or again as a "sub-organisation of the Union", or as a "full-fledged agency". Independently of how it is qualified, there seems to be no doubt that this is an institution which lies fully within the context of Community rules, and not, as has been hypothesised, a totally separate and self-contained entity with regard to both the Community and the Member States.

On this point it has been observed that: "already on the formal level, the rules state that the ESCB implements 'the Community's' monetary policy (Article 105.2) or, again, that the action of 'the Community' includes the definition and conduct of a single monetary and trade policy (Article 4). [...] On a more substantial level, it is moreover indisputable that the ECB finds its basis and its legitimacy in the founding treaty of the EC, which regulates its establishment, functioning and limits of jurisdiction [...]".[100]

Thus the Central Bank may be considered to be an institution which is separate and distinct from the other Community organisms, to which specific tasks, defined by the treaty are assigned, and which is informed with the principles of good conduct and loyal cooperation.

Although this is not the proper place to discuss in depth its tasks and functions, it is however necessary to mention the fact that, as regards the role of prudential supervision of credit institutions and on other financial institutions, it appears to be extremely limited today.[101]

Despite the idea of also entrusting control of the system's stability to the ECB, an idea which emerged during the Treaty of Maastricht negotiations, the final outcome was less ambitious: "Article 105.5 of the Treaty [...] limits itself to providing that the ESCB contribute to the appropriate management of the policies pursued by the competent

98 E. Chiti - C. Franchini, *L'integrazione amministrativa europea*, Bologna, 2003, 78; M.P. Chiti, *Diritto amministrativo europeo*, Milano, 1999, 233; D. O'Keeffe e A. Biondi, *Report on the Implications of the Treaty of Amsterdam for National Ombudsmen and Similar Bodies*, 1998, www.euro-ombudsman.eu.int; P. Bonnor, *The European Ombudsman: A Novel Source of Soft Law in the European Union*, in *European Law Review*, 2000, 39.

99 M. Pifferi, A. Porta, *La Banca Centrale Europea. La politica monetaria nell'area dell'Euro*, Milano, 2003, 5 and ff.

100 A. Malatesta, *La Banca Centrale Europea. Gli aspetti istituzionali della banca centrale della Comunità Europea*, Milano, 2003, 74.

101 K.P. Follak, *International Harmonization of Banking Supervision and Regulation*, in A. Weber (ed.), *Wärung und Wirtschaft*, 379.

authorities. The ESCB/ECB, the article cited above states, "contributes to the good administration of the policies pursued by the relevant authorities as regards prudential supervision over credit institutions and the stability of the financial system. To that end, Article 25 specifies that the ECB may issue opinions and be consulted by the Council and the EU Commission and by the relevant supervisory authorities of the single Member States in the application and implementation of relevant Community legislation. Furthermore, the relevant supervisors have the right to address the ECB "in the field of the application and implementation of Community legislation regarding credit institutions and concerning the stability of the financial system".

These opinions are not, however, binding and, for this reason, many studies are unanimous in declaring the low level of incisiveness of the supervisory function carried out by the central bank.

Thus today the central bank is endowed with essentially consultative functions. This does not however mean that it cannot still be considered as an example of an organism which is part of a collaborative network between Community institutions, Member States and national agencies assigned to supervision of the financial system.

9. The current institutional situation of the supervisory function. The Lamfalussy Committee

As observed above, issues related to supervision in Europe are the result of complex mechanisms that have involved, since the EU was first established, its organs and bodies, in a system which has grown over the years, to achieve today the creation of a single market for banking and financial services, which are often more rationally and effectively subdivided into so-called "financial conglomerates".

The legal basis of reference is the combination of rules resulting from the Treaty and from other Community sources, and from the laws of Member States, in a progressive process of harmonisation that, because of the principle of mutual recognition, has led to the issuing of numerous directives; unquestionably some of the most important are those related to transparency (often referred to in this text).

On this point it has been observed how "the new legislative model has its roots in the current efforts to complete the integration of the EC securities and investment market. Since 1979 the EC has attempted to construct a single market in securities and investment services via the twin pillars of: mutual recognition by the member states of their respective regulatory systems and home Member State control of pan-EC market activity, with all member states subject to minimum standards in the interests of investor protection, systemic stability and effective mutual recognition".[102]

Before proceeding to look at the rules in force today, it is necessary to briefly look at two other important sources of co-ordination, one being mainly aimed at the Community area, the other more international in scope, but also clearly affecting choices made on a

102 N. Moloney, *The Lamfalussy legislative model: a new era for the EC securities and investment services regime*, in *International and Comparative Law Quarterly*, 2003, 509.

Community level. They are respectively the decisions reached by the Lamfalussy Committee in the first case and by the two Basel Councils in the second case.

A step which seems crucial in the progress towards the creation of an efficient reticular system in the area of European financial markets was accomplished in July of 2000 through the institution of the Lamfalussy Committee, the Committee of Wise Men that published the final report on regulation of the European securities markets on 15 February 2001.[103]

The main objective pursued, with the publication of this report, was to rectify the intrinsic difficulty of harmonising the regulatory Community system, by adopting a regulatory approach on four levels and proposing the institution of two committees charged with assisting the European Commission: the European Securities Committee (ESC) and the Committee of European Securities Regulators (CESR).

The structuring of the decision-making process in various phases, during which technical bodies and independent authorities are coordinated in the performance of their supervisory and regulatory functions, renders the system of formation of rules transparent, liberating it from the burden of the cumbersome overlapping of disciplines which it had succumbed to, and saving it from the risk of impending obsolescence. The regulatory approach proposed by the Lamfalussy Committee consists of the following levels:

1) adoption by the Council and European Parliament of directives and regulations containing framework principles;
2) adoption of technical measures to implement the above framework principles. During this phase, the European Commission, on the basis of the provisions contained in the specific directives (level 1), passes on to the Technical Committees the mandates arranging for technical consultancy, thus guaranteeing the approval of a technical opinion made in agreement with the main representatives of the supervisory authority;
3) implementation of a network of supervisory authorities in the securities market sector in order to reinforce cooperation and guarantee effective and uniform transposition of the legislative acts adopted at previous levels;
4) control of application of Community law within Member States by the Commission, by means of strengthened cooperation between Member States, their supervisory authorities and the private sector.

[103] N. Moloney, *op. ult. Cit.*, 518: "Legislation via comitology procedures". E, poco più avanti, ha proceduto ad enucleare i principi nei confronti dei quali il Comitato esorta ad ispirarsi: maintaining confidence in European securities markets; maintaining high levels of prudential supervision; contributing to the efforts of prudential supervisors to censure systemic liability; ensuring appropriate levels of consumer protection proportionate to the different degrees of risk involved; respecting the subsidiarity and proportionality principles; promoting competition and ensuring compliance with the Treaty competition rules; ensuring that regulation is efficient as well as encouraging innovation; and taking account of the European, as well as the wider international dimension of, securities markets".

Moreover, in the Community context, in which the subsidiarity principle plays a key role, the best solution appears to be one which would assign to a central supervisory authority the power to define the main guidelines with which individual authorities of Member States would gradually have to comply.[104]

The objective of effective and widespread surveillance over the banking and financial system appears to be achievable only within a context of enhancement of the competences and the resources of the individual national authorities, to be applied in compliance with the guidelines set by the central authorities.[105]

The main purpose of protecting investors thus emerges also, and particularly, in the Community context, since, during the last few years, a series of directives has been approved, whose inspiring principles are, among others, to ensure market integrity, to raise the quality of services offered and to improve the legal position of investors.[106]

10. Global actors in the financial sector: a system of Chinese boxes

Supervision in the financial sector also has a global dimension. Globalisation comes into play on many levels: in the extreme heterogeneity of the actors which contribute to the structure of the financial system, and in the stratification of standards that those very actors develop and thus are committed to complying with.

Only a few actors in the global arena will be mentioned, those whose activities have an immediate impact on the European system; mention will also be made of some of the mechanisms according to which they are regulated, as an example of a set of dynamics which is fairly complex.

In particular, the corpus of standards developed by the Basel Committee on Banking Supervision is worth mentioning. This committee constitutes only one ramification of the Bank for International Settlements (BIS), which also includes, in addition to the Basel Committee for Banking Supervision, the Committee on Global Financial Systems (CGFS) and the Committee on Payment and Settlement Systems (CPSS).

The provisions laid down at Community level regarding the need for integration in the field of supervision must necessarily be coherent with what has been decided, on an international level, by the Basel Committee.

The Basel Committee constitutes an example, possibly the most important, of a regulatory network which cuts across national powers, as has been noted by M.S Barr and G.P Miller, two experts on global administrative law, applied to the Basel Committee:

104 M. De Bellis, *Gli* standards *globali per i servizi finanziari. Concorrenza e reciproco rafforzamento tra diversi modelli di amministrazione globale*, in S. Cassese, M. Conticelli, *Diritto e amministrazioni nello spazio giuridico globale*, in *Quaderni della Rivista trim. di diritto pubblico*, Milano, 2006, 155.

105 N. Berger, M.A. Mergellina, *Un nouveau système de régulation des marchés des valeurs mobiliéres dans l'Union européenne*, in *Rev. marché comm. Un. Eur.*, 2001, 529.

106 A. Sciarrone Alibrandi, *La sorveglianza sui sistemi di pagamento: evoluzione morfologica, strumenti e limiti*, in *Banca borsa tit. cred.*, 2004, 447; Vella, *Banca Centrale Europea, Banche Centrali Nazionali e vigilanza bancaria: verso un nuovo assetto dei controlli nell'area dell'euro?*, *ivi*, 2002, I, 158; Hahn, *The European Central Bank: key to European Monetary Union or Target?*, in *Common Market Law Review*, 1991, 800.

"The Basel Committee is perhaps the most important example of trans-governmental regulatory network that exercises vast powers, seemingly without any form of democratic accountability. Imagine a club of central bankers meeting secretly in one of Switzerland's wealthiest cities, known for its discretion, its iconographic design and boring bars. The Members of the Basel Committee develop regulations governing the very lifeblood of domestic economies in ways that expand the reach of distant, unaccountable bureaucrats".[107]

The Group of Ten defined global standards, and developed the procedures to be followed by the supervisory authorities in carrying out controls on the correct management of financial operations. This resulted in the first Basel accord, known as Basel I. However the leading figures in world finance met behind closed doors, in great secret, and this was to become its Achilles heel: after subsequent review, the New Agreement would be characterised by more open communication.

The models developed by the Committee were adopted, at national level, by the central and national banks and acted as deterrents for those who strove, on a local level, to hamper and sometimes even to block, the transparency of regulatory procedures. Hence, the interaction between international, transnational and national procedures facilitated the development of rules on behaviour and structures of practice with the purpose of promoting responsibility and legitimacy in the global administrative arena: "At the domestic level, central banks and national bank regulators have enmeshed the Basel standards in the domestic notice and comment rule-making process, enhancing the legitimacy of the international process, through local procedural protections. Moreover, international regulatory processes, including Basel, can in some instances help to reinforce, rather than undermine, domestic norms of accountability and legitimacy, particularly in countries where inside elites block reforms and prevent transparent domestic regulatory processes from occurring. The interaction among these international, transnational and domestic administrative procedures generates norms of behaviour and structures of practice that can help to promote accountability and legitimacy in the global administrative space".[108]

It is as if global law, here embodied by the Basel high officials, manages to erode local particularism and to break down national frontiers, by creating transversal bridges and connections.

The consolidation of the system of banking supervision undoubtedly constitutes the mainstay of the Committee's activities.

During the years after its establishment in 1975, frameworks and models were set up aimed at identifying prudential criteria, both in G10 countries and in those outside the group.

Many publications have been produced, including a list of Fundamental Principles and a Compendium with recommendations, guidelines and requirements issued by the Committee itself.

107 M.S. Barr, G.P. Miller, *Global Administrative Law: The View from Basel, European Journal of International Law*, 2006, 17.

108 M.S. Barr, G.P. Miller, *Global Administrative Law: The View from Basel cit.*, 18.

The principles consist of identification of the requirements for effective banking supervision, and of clarification of the procedural stages, of the procedure of authorisation for carrying out banking activity, of the capital requirements that banks must comply with in order to operate on an international level, and of the controls on the banking sector. This is followed by a detailed description of the supervisory authorities' powers.

However, over the years, banks, regulators and commentators began to manifest their dissatisfaction with an agreement which seemed to be excessively inflexible, not aligned with risks, subject to the regulators' discretion, and to distortions, and also politicised.

Studies showed how the Basel I accord imposed extremely simplified criteria for assessing the quality of investments: capital capacity, number of years' activity, and company name. The Old Basel Accord limited itself to taking into account the company's history, without prescribing any rules on the company's ability to produce revenue.

Hence it became necessary to develop a far more sophisticated system of analysis in order to comprehend the market, which had changed considerably over the years. Furthermore the function of banks had to be modified, from mere savings depository and lending services to real centres of cooperation and integration between businesses and credit institutions, in order to contribute to market growth in an effectively productive manner.

Thus, almost five years after the publication of the first proposal for reform of the system of capital adequacy, imposed by the first Basel Accord and after lengthy consultation between all parties involved, a New Basel Capital Accord was reached, which today is almost in definitive form.[109]

Technically, the operation resulting from Basel II consisted in determining a new solvency ratio, equal to 8%, corresponding to the minimum amount of capital which banks must possess in relation to all their activities weighted according to their credit risk.

The Committee's objective was to achieve the implementation of new regulations on banking supervision, laws that apply on a well established basis only to banks that operate on an international level.

On 26 June 2004 the preliminary work was approved by the governors of the central banks and by those responsible for banking supervision in the Group of Ten countries, within the new framework for the "International Convergence of Capital Measurement and Capital Standards" (commonly referred to as the New Basel Capital Accord or "Basel II"), whose main purpose was to deal with the primary shortcomings in the then-current system of capital capacity.

109 M.S. Barr, G.P. Miller, *Global Administrative Law cit.*, 27: "The Basel Committee has become more accountable over time. The process resulting in the Capital Accords of 1988 were characterized by closed meetings with little or no transparency. Negotiations were conducted without public input, and the final rule was announced [...] as a 'fait accompli'. Domestic implementation in the United States and in the European Union accrued without much additional process. But by time of negotiations over the second accord, Basel, had begun to open up, in part as a response to financial institution pressure for greater transparency and in part because of substantive concerns with first accord had helped to galvanize a debate over new global rules".

Basel II looks back to and expands on the purposes expressed in the first Accord, and constitutes an example of the functioning of international law in the financial sector; the agreement aspires to achieve a framework of common principles, of global standards, which can be applied transversally, to banks operating on an international level, to holding companies of banking groups, to the banks on every level under the head of a banking group and, finally, to the supervisory authorities.

To all the actors of the global legal space, operators in the network – the global arena – in which supranational, infra-national and national relationships criss-cross.

Part 1 of the Agreement reads: "I. 20. This framework will be applied on a consolidated basis to internationally active banks; 21.

The scope of application [...] will include [...] any holding company that is the parent entity within a banking group to ensure that it captures the risk of the whole banking group; 22 [...] to all internationally active banks at every tier within a banking group [...]; 23. Further, as one of the principle objectives of supervision is the protection of depositors, it is essential to ensure that capital recognised in capital adequacy measures is readily available for those depositors. Accordingly, supervisors should test that individual banks are adequately capitalised on a stand-alone basis".

The regulatory framework of Basel II was developed on the basis of a three-pillared structure: the minimal capital requirements (first pillar), the prudential control process (second pillar), and market regulation (third pillar).

It is now important to examine how the construction of the supervisory system implemented in Basel intersects with the regulatory systems which operate today within the European Union. From the standpoint of international administrative law, it is clear that, certainly, there is a close relationship, also in the financial system, between international, European and national players, that are contained one inside the other like Chinese boxes.

11. The financial system of the Europe "box"

The framework of principles formulated in Basel constitutes one of the motors which are driving current legislative modifications in Europe. The overall framework of the financial system's rules requires, indeed, constant adjustment, in order to make it more responsive to risk and to align it to the most sophisticated and up-to-date practices in risk management, thus enhancing European financial stability.

In this context, it is worth mentioning the recent approval of the Resolution of the European Parliament of 11 July 2007 concerning financial services policy for the period 2005–2010 – White Paper.

The recommendations contained in this document may be divided in two large areas: a first area, comprising a series of objectives and comments on the current state of market integration in Europe; a second area on financial integration in its global dimension.[110]

[110] W.M. Isaac, *Somebody Must stop the Runaway Train Basel II*, *American Banker*, 2005, 2A.

The first macro-area includes, for example, the aim of so-called "financial literacy of users", through approval of measures such as access to correct information and impartial advice on investment.

Furthermore, the Parliament praises the work of the European regulatory committees (among others mentioning the Committee of European Securities Regulators (CESR), the Committee of European Banking Supervisors (CEBS) and the Committee of European Insurance Occupational Pensions Supervisors (CEIOPS)), emphasising the importance that an integrated European system of supervisory authorities holds and urging greater coordination. It declares its support for the boards of supervisory authorities responsible for the financial conglomerates that come under various jurisdictions. It also expresses the hope that there will be a convergence of the supervisory authorities' powers, especially as regards sanctions, and the belief that greater cohesion defining supervisors' practice may encourage emergence of a European retail market.[111]

In the second macro-area which the Resolution deals with, the provisions concerning the global impact of integration in the financial sphere are interesting. Point 67 is particularly important; it highlights the need also for the United States supervisory authorities to adopt the Basel standards, with the purpose of developing a Transatlantic partnership, on the basis of common global principles: "[...] it is necessary to develop and reinforce the Transatlantic partnership by enhancing regulatory coordination, highlighting the importance of implementation, on behalf of the United States authorities, of Basel II, as well as mutual recognition of EU and US accounting principles [...] in order to strengthen the coordination of regulation on both sides of the Atlantic and to avoid the useless duplication of rules, or even contrasting rules, for operators of the financial markets".

The White Paper is one of the most recent initiatives revealing the dynamics of the financial system, not only on the European, but also on an international level.

It is another example of the growing awareness of the international dimension of the financial sector.

A global administrative system in which, naturally, the European Central Bank (ECB) plays a prominent role, promoting the harmonisation element as observer on the Basel Committee.

On this occasion, in fact, the ECB manifested its consensus towards the new legislative structure, as the first step in a long-term process, whose final objective is identification of the homogeneous requisites arising from a series of different directives, in a common framework that constitutes the fundamental structure of regulation of the banking system, improving financial integration and making an effective contribution to the further development of the single market.

Naturally, this framework will produce favourable effects on the system of financial integration only when Member States will have actually implemented them.

In this context convergence on regulation must necessarily be completed by convergence on supervision practices.

[111] Www.bis.org/publ/bcbs134.htm, consulted in November 2007.

12. On behaviour standards of financial intermediaries: the transparency principle. Toward the realisation of the third Pillar of Basel II

It is precisely on the topic of transparency in financial operations that some further reflection seems to be necessary.

Both the financial intermediation sector and the banking and insurance sectors are affected by important normative interventions, regarding the transparency of contracts and of financial operations in the broadest sense.

In the banking sector, it is appropriate to mention Directive 2000/12/CE concerning access to the activity and performance of credit institutions, where protection of the client is examined in terms of the bank's stability.

Title V is entirely related to identification of the principles and technical instruments of so-called "prudential supervision", in other words the activity that the competent authorities of Member States must carry out on credit institutions in order to verify the correct application of transparency norms.

In this case as well, in a similar way to the directive concerning supervision over financial conglomerates, the aim is to promote coordination between the various authorities, in order to facilitate the exchange of information between the players active on the market. In particular the 5th subsection of Article 30 requires the implementation of the widest possible "exchange of information, within a Member State, where there are two or more competent authorities in the same Member State, or between Member States, between competent authorities and authorities entrusted with the public duty of supervising other financial organisations and insurance companies, and the authorities responsible for the supervision of financial markets".

Authorities are also endowed with broad sanctioning powers, in their supervisory activity on the transparency of financial operations: if necessary, the directive devolves to the single Member States the task of deciding the sanctions to inflict on credit institutions or directors "which breach laws, regulations or administrative provisions concerning the supervision or pursuit of their activities".

13. Other directives regarding supervision. Implementation of the first and second pillars of Basel II

Having examined provisions concerning transparency and before proceeding to analyse the various models of supervision used in the Member States, as a link between the two, a brief investigation of Community sources regarding supervision in general seems to be appropriate.

One of the main legal sources in this area is Directive n. 2001/34/CE of 28 May 2001 on admission of securities for official listing and the information to be published about these securities; the directive helped to order an area of regulation which had been, up to this moment, extremely disjointed, and thus promoted coordination of the conditions for listing of securities on stock markets in the European Community.

This was followed by approval of Directive 2003/71/CE, with which the European Parliament and Council aimed to overcome the differences between Member States as regards methods and timeframes for the control of information contained in prospectuses; the Directive also requires States to provide themselves with an efficient system of remedies in the event of civil liability arising from the prospectus, and a framework of criminal and administrative sanctions for breach of prospectus obligations.

A third step ahead towards harmonisation is marked by Directive 2003/6/CE of 28 January 2003 against insider dealing and market manipulation.

The Directive specifies that issuing institutions and persons exercising management responsibilities within these companies must communicate insider information, that can affect price trends, to the public and third parties.[112]

Furthermore, on 21 April 2004 Directive 2004/39/CE was approved, concerning the markets for financial instruments; it contains numerous provisions aimed at enhancing the integration and modernisation of the European legal framework, in order to meet the demands of the new context where financial negotiation is carried out.

In particular, considerable space is dedicated to the regulation of relations between authorities responsible for supervision in the single Member States: Article 56 recognises the need for a general duty of collaboration, and devolves to Member States the task of designating a single competent supervisory authority as a point of contact in negotiations.

However, the project of setting up a single supervisory authority, charged with the difficult task of guaranteeing an efficient level of integration of models of financial integration, clashes with the opposing theory of those who highlight how "l'Europe ne s'est pas construite sur la supernationalité, que les structures et les règles financières sont très hétérogènes, que le 'tissu juridique sociologique et linguistique très divers' des Etats de la Communauté serait difficile à gérer par un méga-régulateur européen".

A solution is to be supported which promotes: "une coopération entre un réseau de régulateurs nationaux afin que la régulation des marchés continue à rester un travail réalisé au plus près du terrain et dans le quotidien".[113]

Fundamentally, if the model of a single supervisory authority on a European level seems to be difficult to implement, the trend towards the progressive homogenisation of rules on supervision may be implemented by favouring the creation of technical bodies and intensifying cross-sector cooperation: "the matrix of the structure of European

112 S. Janin, *Le premier cas pratique d'approche "Lamfalussy". Les mesures dìexecution de la Directive sur les opérations d'initiés et les manipulaitons de marché (Abus de marché)*, in *Revue du Marché Commun et de l'Union européenne*, 473, 2003, 658: "La directive sur les abus de marché constitue la première expérience de mise en pratique de l'approche "Lamfalussy", qui est caractérisée par: une différence de procédure d'adoption de "principes essentiels" par rapport à celles suivi pour les "détails techniques", à travers l'introduction de comités et la modification des relations entre Parlement, Conseil et Commission par rapport à la procédure de co-decision; une délimitation précise du champ d'application de ces "détails techniques" par rapport à celui d'une procédure de co-décision.

113 J.P. Valette, *La régulation des marchés financiers cit.*, 201; X. Dieux (ed.), *Les autorités de contrôle des marchés financiers, des assurances et de la concurrence, bilan et perspectives, Actes du Colloque de Bruxelles du 25 mai 2000*, Bruylant, 2002; M.A. Fison-Roche, *Exemple de régulation et de contrôle étrangers, LPA*, 185, 2001, 34; P.A. Gailly, *Vers la création d'une autorité des marchés financiers (AMF): Avant-projet de loi portant réforme des autorités financières*, Rapport présenté à la Chambre de commerce de Paris, 26 September 2002, 11.

regulatory and supervisory co-operation has been (almost) completed with the creation of the Securities Committee and more cross-sector co-operation".[114]

As regards the need, highlighted on many occasions, to implement *cross co-operation* between the different bodies charged with supervision of the correct working of the European market, it must be remembered that the European Parliament and Council adopted Directive 2005/1/CE, with the aim of establishing a new organisational structure for the committees of the financial services sector; this put into effect the recommendations of the Lamfalussy Committee concerning the need to put in place a normative framework articulated on four levels, aimed at increasing the flexibility, transparency and efficiency of the regulation process at Community level in the securities sector.

The Directive primarily introduces some modifications in the organisational structure of the sector Committees (i.e the European Banking Committee, the Committee for European Insurance and Occupational Pensions, and the Committee for Financial Conglomerates), not neglecting however to reaffirm the ever-increasing importance of encouraging co-operation between the Commission, sector Committees and supervisory authorities.

Finally the 2006 Directives n. 48 and 49 need mentioning. They implement the 1st and 2nd pillars of the Basel Accord.

Although based on the "Basel II" regulatory framework, the new framework regulating capital adequacy in the European Union has some different features.

Firstly, as regards profile, while the Basel II framework is aimed at banks operating on an international level, the European framework will be applied to all credit institutions and investment companies, regardless of their level of complexity or sophistication.

Secondly, the European framework aims to guarantee that prudential standards are adequate to the risks taken. Finally, and of most interest to us, the European framework allows greater cooperation and better coordination between supervisory authorities compared to the Basel accords regulation, thus reinforcing the role of the authority responsible for consolidated supervision.

114 K. Lannoo, *The Incomplete European Market for Financial Services cit.*, 249. See also Y.V. Avgerinos, *EU Financial Market Supervision Revisited: The European Securities Regulator, Jean Monnet Working Paper*, NYU School of Law, 2003, n. 7, "in the future, the issue of a single EU regulator cannot be avoided by the markets and their participants. Acting in a single currency and unified se curities market environment, the new regime would have the advantage of the status quo of a bigger body of common regulations, lower costs and greater flexibility. On the other hand, the lack of a single supervisor can impede competition and innovation beneficial to financial firms, issues and consumers. Europe has a responsibility to pursue financial institutional reform; not only for its own benefit, but also for the good of its neighbours – helping the global economic growth, and promoting international cooperation beyond its own borders to ensure that globalisation works for the benefit of all". V.E.P. Gardener, *Theory and practice in banking supervision: Some Reflections*, IES, *Institute of European Finance*, 1986, 2; D. Llewellyn, *The Regulation and Supervision of Financial Institutions, Gilbart Lectures on Banking*, 1986; C. Goodhart, *Financial regulation: Why, How and Where Now?*, London, Routledge, 1998, 189; G. Walker, *International Banking Regulation: Law, Policy and Practice*, London, 2001, 1; M. Levitt, *Does Europe Want a Single Market?*, in *The Financial Regulator*, 2001, 4, 20; S. Ciardi, *La vigilanza nell'era della BCE*, e G. Marcucci, *Vigilanza: stratificazione istituzionale neazionale e prospettive d'impatto europee (Il caso Italia)*, in F. Belli – V. Santoro (eds.), *La Banca Centrale Europea*, CE.DI.B. Studi di diritto e legislazione bancaria, Milano, 2003, 483, 457.

Usually this is embodied by the national supervisory authority of the Member State where the parent company of a group with companies in a number of Member States has its corporate domicile.

This authority is responsible for the highest level of supervision of a European group with the above characteristics.

In conclusion, it is difficult to disagree with the view that the rules on cooperation in supervision constitute the keystone of the Community regulatory framework based on the two pillars of minimum harmonisation and mutual recognition.[115]

However, although there are grounds for optimism regarding the attainment of an increasingly sophisticated level of cooperation, understandable caution applies as regards the difficulties still remaining in adjusting the current system in which the supervisory authorities have jurisdiction on a national basis in order to keep up with the growing integration of the European financial market.

115 F. Recine, *La direttiva relativa ai mercati degli strumenti finanziari (MiFID): nuove regole sulla cooperazione tra le autorità di vigilanza*, in *Diritto della banca e del mercato finanziario*, 2006, 230.

Chapter 3

CHAPTER 3. THE GERMAN SYSTEM

Section 1. Powers

1. *Independent Administrative Authorities in the German system*

The origin of the independent authority structural model may be traced back to the Conference held at the Berlin Chamber of Commerce by Carl Schmitt in 1930, at which it was declared that the German central bank, as well as other bodies such as the Railways, were "neutral" organs of administration of the economy with regards to government policy.[116]

The problem of the constitutional basis of independent organisations in Germany lies mainly in identifying a regulation that combines the democratic principle and devolution of powers to external and independent organs.

In other words, the main issue regards establishing the way in which the constitutionally required principle of democracy may be reconciled with the need for delegation of powers to expert bodies which are independent from day-to-day politics. Pursuant to Article 20 GG all State authority has to emanate from the people. Therefore, a continuous chain of legitimacy between the sovereign people and the state power must be shown generally for all powers.

This means that delegation of powers must receive constitutional coverage and is therefore only legitimate within the bounds of the constitution. In the tension between democratic principle and authorities' independence from political power, the democratic principle still prevails, so that generally "a legal form which states dependency on government is chosen even if in practice the principle of non intervention prevails".[117]

In the delicate balance between the requirements of independence and the requirements of conformity to the constitution, there is a tendency towards the creation of a system in which the independent authorities, in regulating the system's sensitive

116 C. Schmitt, *Das Problem der innerpolitischen Neutralitaet*, in *Verfassungsgericht Aufsätze aus den Jahren* 1924–1925, Berlin, 1958, 41.

117 A. Van Aaken, Independent Administrative Agencies in Germany, in www.dirittoamministrativo.jus.unitn.it, consulted in November 2007.

sectors, are bound to comply with the rule of law. Thus, upon closer examination, the independent authorities too, like all the administrative authorities of the German system, are obliged to observe the rule of law, as they are bound "to the statutes and the law" ("*an Gesetz und Recht gebunden*").[118]

2. *The German financial system from a functional perspective*

Analysis of the problems connected with regulation of the German financial system from, as it were, a "functional" perspective, aimed, in other words, at the precise identification of the tasks and functions assigned to the market operators, as direct recipients of regulatory dispositions, requires an introduction on the institutional nature and characteristics of these intermediaries.[119]

The structure of the German financial system, as in other countries, consists of three main areas of regulation: the banking sector[120], the sector of non-banking financial intermediaries (where a considerable role is played by the insurance market) and the sector of financial intermediaries in the narrow sense.

In listing the main characteristics of the banking system, let us look at the primary features that have been identified within it.[121] Firstly, this is a system dominated by "universal banks" in the true sense of the term, that is, not based on the activity of mere "financial conglomerates" but rather on the work of real credit institutions, provided with a well-defined structure and organisation. Secondly, the primary objective of banking activity is not simply related to the principle of "profit-maximisation", because banks offer many alternative services to clients, including deposit taking and lending. Thirdly, competition occurs mainly at an interbank level and not so much between groups. Fourthly, the undeniable predominance of banking institutions in Germany has an inevitable effect on the country's gross domestic product. Finally, even if the primary

118 B. Rudolf, *The Enforcement of Judgements Against Public Authorities in the Federal Republic of Germany, European Public Law*, 2001 who states that "the importance of the executive's being bound to the statutes and the law cannot be underestimated [...]. Given the historic experience of the national-socialist rule with its blatant disregard of the rule of law, this principle has assumed a central position in the self image of the Federal republic of Germany. An administrative authority that intentionally disregards the law leaves the common ground of societal consensus". For a general framework on administrative law in Germany see O. Mayer, *Theorie des französischen Verwaltungsrechts*, 1886, 2; see also C.F. Gerber, *Über öffentliches Recht*, 1852; G. Jellinek, *Gesetz und Verordnung, Staatsrechtliche Untersuchungen auf Rechtgeschichtlicher und Rechtvergleichender Grundlage*, Tübingen, 1919; V.E. Orlando, *Giorgio Jellinek e la storia del diritto pubblico generale*, 1949, Milano; ID., *Diritto pubblico generale. Scritti varii (1881–1940) coordinati in sistema*, Milano, 1940.

119 J.P. Kranen, R.H. Schmidt, *The German Financial System*, Oxford University Press, New York, 2004; V. Alexander – M. Bohl, *Das Finanzsystem in Deutschland*, in J. Von Hagen and J.H. Von Stein, *Obst/Hintner Geld, Bank und Börsenwesen*, IV ed., Stuttgart, 2000, 447; M. Tyrell, *Kapitalmärkte und Banken – Formen der Informationsverarbeitung als konstitutives Merkal*, Wiesbaden, 2003; A. Winkler, *Wirtschaftswachstum und Finanzsystementwicklung*, Mimeo, 2001.

120 See BaFin papers: *Geschichte der Bankenaufsicht, Geschichte der Versicherungsausicht, Geschichte* der Wertpapieraufsicht, in www.bafin.de, consulted in April 2008 and also *Basel Committee on Banking Supervision, Working Paper n. 14, Studies on the Validation of Internal Rating Systems, Basel*, 2005.

121 J.P. Krahnen, R.H. Schmidt, *The German Financial System cit.*, 29.

German banks do not seem to be performing a radically different activity from the primary world banks, they clearly differ in the above-mentioned significant number of services that they offer, among which lending and deposit taking predominate.[122]

Non-financial intermediaries divide into two macro-categories: investment and insurance companies.

The close connection between the banking system and the insurance system is illustrated by the fact that more than half of the funds originating from the insurance sector are invested in loans and bank bonds. On this point, it has been said that "there are close connections between the insurance and banking industries which manifest themselves in cross-holdings of equity and seats on the respective and supervisory boards".

It is precisely in order to make these cross-sector relations and exchanges more transparent that legislation was enacted to regulate the system and assign supervision of the banking and insurance sectors to a single authority, thus allowing more effective control of the workings of these two systems.

From 1 May 2002, BaFin was assigned the functions of supervision of the banking and insurance sectors: "Zum 1 Mai 2002 ist das BAV mit den damaligen Bundesaufsichtsamptern für das Kreditwesen (BAKred) und den Wertpaperhandel (BAWe) zur Bundesanstalt für Finanzdienstleistungsaufsicht (BaFin) verschmolzen worden".[123]

In a sense, it may be said that this legislative change was made necessary, since a trend towards a return to a unitary vision of the different market sectors had already been initiated by the market itself and, specifically, by the process of financial innovation which had developed within it.

Scholars have made in-depth studies of this process of integration, which is particularly visible in Germany, but now also common to the other main European systems. Its essence has been identified in the widespread proliferation of financial instruments and in their ever-growing need for uniformity: "Financial innovation has in fact enabled many categories of intermediaries, belonging to different sectors, to invade [...] market sectors which the law had reserved to other intermediaries. A typical example of this phenomenon is that of the massive involvement of banks in intermediary activities with new financial products, essentially the same as securities".[124]

Finally, in extremely simplified terms, it is also possible to distinguish a number of different subsystems or market segments in the financial sector in the narrow sense: the

122 J.P. Krahnen – R.H. Schmidt, *TheGerman Financial System cit.*, 34.

123 §4.4. Finanzdienstleistunsaufsichtsgesetz (FinDAG) 22 April 2002, *BGBl* I, 2002, 1310.

124 D. Regoli, *Mercati finanziari in diritto comparato*, in *Dig. disc. priv., Sez. comm.*, vol. IX, Torino, 1993, 410: "L'innovazione finanziaria ha infatti consentito a diverse categorie di intermediari appartenenti a comparti diversi di invadere [...] comparti di mercato per legge riservati ad altri intermediari. Un esempio tipico di quest'ultimo fenomeno è quello della massiccia partecipazione delle banche ad attività di intermediazione di nuovi prodotti finanziari, sostanzialmente assimilabili ai valori mobiliari"; A. Franklin, R. Herring, *Banking regulation versus securities market regulation*, Wharton Financial Institution Center, Working Paper, 2001; M. Höpner, G. Jackson, *An emerging market for corporate control? The Mannesmann takeover and German corporate governance*, Max Planck Institut für Gesellschaftsforschung Discussion Paper, 2001, Münich.

official market (*amtlicher Markt*), the semi-official market (*gerekter Markt*) and finally, the over- the-counter market (*Freiverkher*).[125]

This sector, as happens in the insurance sector, also seems to be considerably permeated by the banking sector. This phenomenon, on one hand, constitutes a strong incentive towards ever-increasing integration and homogenisation of the market segments. On the other, it poses the risk, much feared by experts, that the excessive inflexibility of the one will affect the correct functioning and flexibility of the others: "As far as the banking sector as the backbone of the German financial system is concerned, regulation seems to have at least delayed adjustment, and hence reduced the capability to meet these challenges, in three ways. First, the lack of competition from financial markets probably reduced pressures for banks to price individual products and services – and in particular loans – appropriately. Second, cheap access to retail funds enabled decoupling of lending rates from market interest rates, thereby creating room to lend at sub-market rates. Third, public ownership has complicated consolidation and cemented cost structures that lower bank profitability and impair the capacity to assume risk".[126]

On the basis of what has been said so far, the essentially tripartite nature of the German supervisory framework is clear, made up of a normative structure that disciplines the three sectors systemically, with the main purpose of integrating them.[127]

3. *Prospectus transparency obligations: an example of normative systematisation in finance*

In all regulation of investment markets, control of information and transparency of the market plays a primary role in the protection of investors: this constitutes the main objective of regulation of the market.

In concrete terms, the need for transparency is expressed within the different national systems through the prescription of certain duties to inform, on the part of the companies

125 K.D. Dehlinger, *Vertragliche Marktsegmentregulierung am Wertpapierbörsen*, Baden Baden, 2003, 36: "Das Prinzip des Numerus Clausus der Marktsegmente ist im Grundsatz so zu verstehen, daß der Wertpapierhandel unter dem Nach der Börse nur im amtlichen Markt, im geregelten Markt und im Freiverkehr stattfindet"; T. Baums, *Corporate governance in Germany, system and current developments*, Universität Osnabrück Institut für Handels-und Wirtschaftsrecht Working, Paper 70, 2000.

126 D. Domanski, *The impact of financial regulation on financial structures on postwar Germany cit.*, 33. H. Hempell, *Testing for competition among German banks, Economic Research Centre of the Bundesbank Discussion Paper*, 04/2002, 21.

127 H. Maurer, *Allgemeines Verwaltungsrecht*, Verlag C.H. Beck, München, 2004, 534: "Die Begriffe Organ und Organwalter sind in der Rechtslehre zur systematischen Erfassung der funktionellen Zusammenhänge der Verwaltungsorganisation entwickelt worden [...]. Die 'behörde' ist ein Zentralbegriff des Verwaltungsorganisationrechts wie bereits ihre vorzugweise Verwendung in der Gesetzbung, Verwaltung und Literatur zeigt [...]. Behörden im organisatorischen Sinne sind die in die staatliche Verwaltungshierarchie eingeordneten Organe sowie die Vollzugsorgane der nichtstaatlichen Verwaltungsträger, also etwa der Regierungspräsident, der Finanzamt, der Bürgermeister, der Dekan der Fakultät einer Universität. Behörden im funktionellen Sinne sind dagegen alle Organe, wenn und soweit sie zur hoheitlichen Durchführung konkreter Verwaltungsmaßnahmen im Außenverhältnis berufen sind".

who issue securities for the public, and through the establishment of control mechanisms aimed at guaranteeing information for investors.

In the regulation of financial markets, it is the German system that was the first to approve rules defining the duty of issuing companies, to compile and publish informative prospectuses in order to gain admittance to official listing on the stock market and to sell financial instruments on the market.[128]

The first law on this area dates back to 1896, the year in which the *Börsengesetz* was approved. This law is still in force, although with important modifications; the most substantial is probably that introduced by the *Drittes Finanzmarktförderungsgesetz,* in force since May 1998.[129]

Around this prominent as well as consolidated body of law we find many other laws.[130] Many came into being as a consequence of implementation of community dispositions. Today the legal area of *Prospekthaftung*, or informative prospectus liability, constitutes a fundamental component in the German financial system.[131]

3.1. The notion of informative prospectus

Before looking at prospectus liability, generally related to problems concerning financial transparency, we will define the notion of prospectus.

Firstly, however, it is important to mention that such liability, disciplined both by special laws and by ordinary law, has its foundation in the concept of culpa in contrahendo: "Im Deutschland wird die Prospekthaftung sowohl allgemein-zivilrechtlich (bürgerlich-rechtlich) als auch spezialgesetzliche geregelt. Die allgemein-zivilrechtliche Prospekthaftung basiert im Wesenlich auf den Grundlagen der culpa in contrahendo".[132]

In particular, an attempt was made to harmonise the general regulation of securities trading with a practice which has taken hold in the *grauer Kapitalmarkt,* the grey capital

128 H. Roller, *Die Prospekthaftung im Englischen und im Deutschen Recht,* Berlin, 1991; C. Benicke, *Prospektpflicht und Prospekthaftung bei grenzüberschreitenten Emissionem*, in *Festschrift für Erik Jayme*, Münich, 2004, 25.

129 Law 27 March 1998. Gesetz zur wietern Fortenwicklung des Finanzplatzes Deutschland - *Drittes Finanzmarktförderungsgesetz* (3 FFG), in *BGBI*, I, 529. The Law follows the Gesetz über den Wertpapierhandel und zur Änderung börsenrechtlicher und wertpapierrecht Vorschriften - 2 FFG, 26 July 1944, in *BGBI*, I, 1749, amended several times and finally by *Bilanzkontrollgesetz* on 15 November 2004, *BGBI*, I, 2004, 3408. The latter introduced measure to strengthen the stakeholders' trust in the market. Furthermore, G. D'Alfonso, *Responsabilità da prospetto informativo. Confronto tra evoluzione legislativa,* elaborazione giurisprudenziale e dottrinale nel sistema italiano e tedesco, Napoli, 2002; ID., *La tutela del risparmio in Italia e in Germania, tra "disegni" e realizzazioni*, in *Studium Juris*, 2005, 401.

130 Amongst the most relevant: Gesetz über die Integrierte Finanzdienstleistungsaufsicht - FinDAG 25 April 2002, in *BGBI*, I, 2001, 1310; Gesetz zur weiteren Fortentwicklung des Finanzplatzes Deutschland (4 FFG), 21 June 2002, ivi, I, 2002, 2010; Investmentmodernisierungsgesetz del 1° gennaio 2002, ivi, I, 2003, 2676.

131 J. Vortmann (ed.), *Prospekthaftung und Anlageratung*, 2000, Stuttgart, 201.

132 U. Ehricke, *Prospekt-und Kapitalmarktinformationshaftung in Deutschland*, in K.J. Hopt, H. Christoph Voigt, *Prospekt- und Kapitalmarktinformationshaftung, Max Planck Institut für ausländisches und Internationales Privatrecht*, Mohr Siebeck, Tübingen, 2005, 190.

market, whereby entrepreneurs, not being subject to institutional forms of control, were not punished except by means of the expedient of *culpa in contrahendo*; to do this, the *Angerschutzverbesserungsgesetz*[133] was approved, a law to improve the protection of investors.

This law, relating specifically to forms of investor protection in the financial market area, and implementing Articles 1 n.3 and 11 of the Market Abuse Directive, provides that: "leaving aside the competencies of the judiciary, each Member State designates a single administrative authority to oversee application of the provisions implemented under this directive".

It modifies the concept of financial instruments and, in addition, extends the functions of the supervisory authority, the *Bundesanstalt für Finanzdienstleitungsaufsicht (BaFin)*.

The supporting structure of the system of rules on financial matters illustrated seems, therefore, to consist of rules regarding investor protection: as mentioned above, as early as 1896, with the *Börsengesetz*, the main purpose of legislation passed was to provide for a series of rules to protect the transparency of market operations, safeguards which during the course of the century, have been gradually perfected, up to the establishment of an authority in charge of ensuring the fairness of financial operations.[134]

4. *Establishment and aims of the Bundesanstalt für Finanzdienstleistungs-aufsicht (BaFin)*

Ever since it was founded, in May 2002, the Federal Financial Supervisory Authority (*Bundesanstalt für Finanzdientleistungsaufsicht, BaFin*) has exercised the integrated functions of supervising banking and finance, insurance, and securities trading. It was established as an independent public law body, that however maintains ties with the Ministry of Finance, whose legal and functional supervision it is subject to.

BaFin is thus a federal authority, that operates under the Federal Ministry of Finance. This means that it is subordinate only to the highest federal body, that is the Federal Ministry of Finance, whose authority it comes under, and which has jurisdiction over all federal territory.

Independence from the federal government means essentially independence from the Ministry of Finance in terms of funding, because it is financed by the businesses and institutions that are subject to its supervision.[135]

Even the location of the supervisory authority, inside the Ministry of Finance building in the centre of Bonn, reveals the true nature of a body which, although independent, still remains within the Ministry structure: its employees are part of the *BundesMinisterium der Finanzen* and they take their meals at the same canteen as Ministry employees.

133 *Gesetz zur Verbesserung des Angelegerschutzes – AnSVG* 28 October 2003, in *BGBI*, I, 2004, 2630.

134 V.H. Williamson, *Boost for Germany's Financial Role: Federal Agency Three Regulator Bodies to be Merged into a single Authority from May 1*, in *Fin. Times*, Apr. 3, 2002, 12.

135 C. Di Capua, *Il sistema bancario tedesco*, in *Quaderni di Ricerche realizzati nell'ambito della ricerca "Verso un sistema bancario e finanziario europeo"*, a cura dell'Ente per gli Studi Monetari, Bancari e Finanziari Luigi Einaudi, n. 56, 2003.

BaFin was established following approval of the FinDAG[136], on 22 April 2002, with the specific purpose of unifying the three market supervisory functions (banking, insurance, and securities) under a single federal body. It thus merged the federal supervisory offices for the credit system (*Bundesauftsichtamt für das Kreditwesen – BAKred*), for the insurance system (*Bundesaufsichtamt für das Versicherungswesen – BAV*) and for the financial products trade (*Bundesaufsichtamt für Wertpapierhandel*).[137]

Regarding this last point, it has been observed that: "the BaFin has three main supervisory objectives: its paramount aim is to ensure the functioning of the entire financial industry in Germany. From this objective, two others can be inferred: to safeguard the solvency of banks, financial services institutions and insurance undertakings – which in the past was mainly a function of the BAKred and the BAV – and to protect clients and investors".[138]

Fundamentally, the main objectives that BaFin pursues, in a perspective of general supervision and in defence of the public interest, relate to supervision of the stock market as a whole, both in terms of the transparency and solvency of banks, and of the protection of investors.

BaFin operates in the public interest. Its main objective is to guarantee the correct working, stability and integrity of the German financial system, so as to allow clients, as well as insurance companies and investors, to have complete trust in the system. In addition to the general function of ensuring supervision over the solvency of institutions subject to its controls, BaFin is also responsible for ensuring that banks, financial institutions and insurance companies fulfil their duties appropriately.

Through its activity of market supervision, BaFin also encourages the adoption of standards of practice and behaviour, with the aim of maintaining the confidence of investors in the financial market.

One of the objectives that BaFin pursues is the struggle against the system of so-called "unauthorised financial business".[139]

5. *BaFin's Structure*

BaFin comprises three distinct organisational units, known as Directorates: the unit assigned to banking supervision (*Bankenaufsicht*), one assigned to insurance system supervision (*Versicherungsaufsicht*) and lastly one charged with supervision of the

136 *Gesetz über die integrierte Finanzdienstungfsicht 22 April* 2002, *BGBI*, I, 1310.

137 K.D. Dehlinger, *Vertragliche Marktsegmentregulierung an Wertpapierbörsen*, Baden Baden, 2003.

138 K.K. Mwenda, *Legal aspects of Unified Financial Services Supervision in Germany*, in *German Law Journal*, 2003, 4, 10.

139 See pag. 9 *Annual Report*, 2006, Bafin, on www.bafin.de/jahresbericht/2006/kapitel_VIII_en.pdf: "BaFin may also enforce measures against companies that are unwittingly involved in unauthorised business, for instance taking recourse to their regular services. During the year under review, BaFin issued instructions to two involved companies".

financial system in a strict sense and asset management (*Wertpapieraufsicht/Asset Management*).[140]

The first unit is divided into four departments, each respectively responsible for oversight of large banks and certain credit institutions (*Aufsicht über Großbanken und ausgewählte Kreditbanken*), of Länder banks, savings banks and rural banks (*Aufsicht über Landesbanken, Sparkassen und Bauskassen*), with supervision of banks granting credit, of special and of regional banks (*Aufsicht über Kreditbanken, Regionalbanken und Spezialbanken*) and, lastly, with supervision over credit institutions and the lawfulness of cooperative shareholding models (*Aufsicht über Kreditinstitute in der Rechtsform der eigetragenen Genossenschaft*).

The second unit is composed of five department structures. The first is charged with carrying out general functions in the insurance system, such as establishing insurance conditions, as well as management of the health insurance system (*Grundsatzfragen der Versicherungsaufsicht; aufsicht über Krankenversicherungsunternehmen*). The second oversees the life insurance system (*Aufsicht über Lebensversicherungsunternehmen und Sterbenkassen*). The third oversees damage insurance and national insurance groups (*Aufsicht über Schaden und Unfall V-U, Nationale Versicherungsgruppe*); the fourth, international insurance groups and financial conglomerates (*Internationale Versicherungsgruppen und Finanzkonglomerate*). The last department oversees pension insurance systems (*Bertriebliche Altersorgung; aufsicht über Pensionkassen und Pensionfonds*).

The third directorate consists of four departments. The first has similar functions to those of the first insurance department, in other words with responsibilities for identifying general principles and conditions of the financial supervision system (*Grundsatzfragen der Wertpapieraufsicht*). The second has oversight of insider trading and forms of publicity for investments, as well as stock exchange competencies (*Insideruberwachung, Ad-Hoc-Publizität; Director's dealing; Borsen kompetenz-zentrum*). The third is charged with supervision over the correct application of laws concerning credit (*Aufsicht über FDI nach KWG und WpHG*). The last department is responsible for supervision over investment funds (*Investmentfonds*).[141]

140 C. Schiedermair, "*3L3*" – *European financial supervisors cooperate across sector boundaries*, pubblicato in *Q3/07, Bafin Quarterly, 3rd Quarter Edition* 2007, *Issued by the Federal Financial Supervisory*, p. 4; see also *BaFin, 2005, Jahresbericht der Bundesanstalt für Finanzdienstleistungsaufsicht, DruckVerlag Kettler GmbH, Bönen*, Bonn und Frankfurt am Main, 2006.

141 Www.bafin.de/bafin/organigramm_en.pdf.

6. *Functions*

6.1. BaFin's powers under the Financial Instruments Law (Wertpapierhandelgesetz - WpHG)

One of the main laws governing BaFin's functions is the law on financial instruments (*Wertpapierhandelgesetz - WpHG*)[142], enacted in 1998 but subsequently amended in the sections regarding supervision.[143] We will to look at part II, especially sections 3–10 of this law, regulating BaFin's powers and functions. Section 3 states that the authority has general responsibility for supervision under the law, and assigns to BaFin a general power to act in order to prevent or eliminate any risks which may arise in the financial system.[144]

The Authority oversees and monitors compliance with laws safeguarding the proper functioning of the market, and may provide any instructions required to ensure their implementation. It also holds the power of prohibiting or suspending the circulation of financial products on the market.[145] In order to fulfil its supervisory functions over the financial sector, BaFin also exercises powers of so-called inspectional supervision: it can gather information, and request documentation, to the extent that it deems necessary for effective monitoring of possible breaches of the law.

In coordination with this inspectional activity, BaFin must immediately inform the public prosecutor[146] in the event that there is evidence that an offence has been committed under section 38 of the same law.[147]

142 Wertpapierhandelgesetz - WpHG, in der Fassung der Bekanntmachung vom 9. September 1998, in *BGBl.*, I, 2708.

143 *Handelsgesetzbuch, Wertpapierhandelgesetz*, 44. Auflage, 2006, Becktexte in Dtv, München.

144 §3 (1) Wertpapierhandelgesetz - WpHG *cit.*: "§3 *Aufgaben und Befugnisse.* (1) Die Bundesanstalt für Finanzdienstleistungsaufsicht (Bundesanstalt) übt die Aufsicht nach den Vorschriften dieses Gesetzes aus. Sie hat im Rahmen der ihr zugewiesenen Aufgaben Missständen entgegenzuwirken, welche die ordnungsgemäße Durchführung des Handels mit Finanzinstrumenten oder von Wertpapierdienstleistungen oder Wertpapiernebendienstleistungen beeinträchtigen oder erhebliche Nachteile für den Finanzmarkt bewirken können. Sie kann Anordnungen treffen, die geeignet und erforderlich sind, diese Missstände zu beseitigen oder zu verhinder".

145 §3 (2) Wertpapierhandelgesetz - WpHG *cit.*: "(2) Die Bundesanstalt überwacht die Einhaltung der Verbote und Gebote dieses Gesetzes und kann Anordnungen treffen, die zu ihrer Durchsetzung geeignet und erforderlich sind. Sie kann den Handel mit einzelnen oder mehreren Finanzinstrumenten vorübergehend untersagen [...]".

146 §3 (5) Wertpapierhandelgesetz - WpHG *cit.*: "5) Die Bundesanstalt hat Tatsachen, die den Verdacht einer Straftat nach §38 begründen, der zuständigen Staatsanwaltschaft unverzüglich anzuzeigen. Sie kann die personenbezogenen Daten der Betroffenen, gegen die sich der Verdacht richtet oder die als Zeugen in Betracht kommen, der Staatsanwaltschaft übermitteln, soweit dies für Zwecke der Strafverfolgung erforderlich ist.

147 §3 (3) Wertpapierhandelgesetz - WpHG *cit.*: "(3) Die Bundesanstalt kann von jedermann Auskünfte, die Vorlage von Unterlagen und die Überlassung von Kopien verlangen sowie Personen laden und vernehmen, soweit dies auf Grund von Anhaltspunkten für die Überwachung der Einhaltung eines Verbots oder Gebots dieses Gesetzes erforderlich ist [...].Sie kann insbesondere die Angabe von Bestandsveränderungen in Finanzinstrumenten sowie Auskünfte über die Identität weiterer Personen,

If the Authority believes that the investigation is not being carried out according to legal requirements, it may request the publication of a report or a statement providing an account of the main phases of the preliminary enquiry.[148]

This law specifies, in addition, that any kind of objection or protest against the abovementioned measures can have no delaying effect.[149]

The last of the authority's sanctionative powers is found in the provision that refers to the principle of international cooperation, and permits disclosure of information regarding persons under investigation only for the purpose of guaranteeing *International Zusammenarbeit* (international cooperation): "(10) Die Bundesanstalt darf ihr mitgeteilte personenbezogene Daten nur zur Erfllung ihrer aufsichtlichen Aufgaben und für Zwecke der Internationalen Zusammenarbeit nach Maßgabe des §7 speichern, verändern und nutzen".[150]

6.2. The advisory committee

Other regulations, aside from those concerning the powers which BaFin is invested with, relate to the establishment within the Authority of an advisory committee consisting of representatives from each *Land*, who are assisted, if necessary, also by representatives from the Ministry of Finance, of Justice, of Economy and Labour, as well as representatives from the German Federal Bank. The committee may also consult with experts on securities, on the stock exchange and on economics.[151]

The committee carries out supervision and provides the supervisory authority with opinions in the following ways: 1. through issuing opinions and guidelines concerning BaFin's supervisory activity; 2. through consultancy in the area of supervision of stock market institutions and institutions that trade in financial instruments; 3. through

insbesondere der Auftraggeber und der aus Geschäften berechtigten oder verpflichteten Personen, verlangen".

148 §3 (5) Wertpapierhandelgesetz – WpHG *cit.*: "(6) Die Bundesanstalt kann eine nach den Vorschriften dieses Gesetzes gebotene Veröffentlichung oder Mitteilung auf Kosten des Pflichtigen vornehmen, wenn die Veröffentlichungs- oder Mitteilungspflicht nicht, nicht richtig, nicht vollständig oder nicht in der vorgeschriebenen Weise erfüllt wird".

149 §3 (7) Wertpapierhandelgesetz – WpHG *cit.*: "(7) Widerspruch und Anfechtungsklage gegen Maßnahmen nach den Absätzen 1-*bis* 4 und 6 haben keine aufschiebende Wirkung". The following provisions contains procedural guarantees, such as the possibility to be assisted by an attorney: "(9) Der zur Erteilung einer Auskunft Verpflichtete kann die Auskunft auf solche Fragen verweigern, deren Beantwortung ihn selbst oder einen der in §383 Abs. 1 Nr. 1- *bis* 3 der Zivilprozessordnung bezeichneten Angehörigen der Gefahr strafgerichtlicher Verfolgung oder eines Verfahrens nach dem Gesetz über Ordnungswidrigkeiten aussetzenwürde. Der Verpflichtete ist über sein Recht zur Verweigerung der Auskunft zu.

150 §3 (10) Wertpapierhandelgesetz – WpHG *cit.* See *amplius* in the next paragraphs.

151 §5 (1) Wertpapierhandelgesetz – WpHG *cit.*: "§5 (1) Bei der Bundesanstalt wird ein Wertpapierrat gebildet. Er besteht aus Vertretern der Länder. Die Mitgliedschaft ist nicht personen gebunden. Jedes Land entsendet einen Vertreter. An den Sitzungen können Vertreter der Bundesministerien der Finanzen, der Justiz und für Wirtschaft und Arbeit sowie der Deutschen Bundesbank teilnehmen. Der Wertpapierrat kann Sachverständige insbesondere aus dem Bereich der Börsen, der Marktteilnehmer, der Wirtschaft und der Wissenschaft anhören [...]".

supervisory activity on the correct division of competencies between BaFin and the authorities charged with supervision of the markets as well as cooperation between them.[152]

The advisory committee may also make recommendations regarding general progress on supervisory operations by BaFin which, in turn, compiles an annual report on its supervisory activity, on progress made in this activity and also on international security and cooperation.[153] The committee is convened at least once a year by BaFin's President and, in the event that one third of its members request it, each member has the right to contribute to the committee's advisory activity.[154]

6.3. On duties of international and national cooperation between supervisory authorities

The WpHG provisions include a standard clause on the duties of cooperation between authorities charged with oversight of the securities market, cooperation which must be in place both on a national and international level. Section 7 of the law specifies a list of duties of cooperation with authorities that operate abroad: as regards supervision of financial instruments and markets, subsection 1 of section 7 states that BaFin must cooperate with the supervisory authorities of other Member States of the European Community and of the states which are parties to the Agreement on the European Economic Area.[155]

152 §5 (2) del WpHG: "(2) Der Wertpapierrat wirkt bei der Aufsicht mit. r berät die Bundesanstalt, insbesondere 1. bei dem Erlass von Rechtsverordnungen und der Aufstellung von Richtlinien für die Aufsichtstätigkeit der Bundesanstalt, 2. hinsichtlich der Auswirkungen von Aufsichtsfragen auf die Börsen- und Marktstrukturen sowie den Wettbewerb im Handel mit Finanzinstrumenten 3. bei der Abgrenzung von Zuständigkeiten zwischen der Bundesanstalt und den Börsenaufsichtsbehörden sowie bei Fragen der Zusammenarbei".

153 §5 (3) Wertpapierhandelgesetz – WpHG *cit.* Così recita il §5 (3) del WpHG: "Der Wertpapierrat kann bei der Bundesanstalt Vorschläge zur allgemeinen Weiterentwicklung der Aufsichtspraxis einbringen. Die Bundesanstalt berichtet dem Wertpapierrat mindestens einmal jährlich über die Aufsichtstätigkeit, die Weiterentwicklung der Aufsichtspraxis sowie über die internationale Zusammenarbeit [...]".

154 §5 (3) Wertpapierhandelgesetz – WpHG *cit.*: "[...] §5 (3) Der Wertpapierrat wird mindestens einmal jährlich vom Präsidenten der Bundesanstalt einberufen. Er ist ferner auf Verlangen von einem Drittel seiner Mitglieder einzuberufen. Jedes Mitglied hat das Recht, Beratungsvorschläge einzubringen".

155 §7 (1) Wertpapierhandelgesetz – WpHG *cit.* "§7 Zusammenarbeit mit zuständigen Stellen im Ausland (1) Der Bundesanstalt obliegt die Zusammenarbeit mit den für die Überwachung von Finanzinstrumenten und von Märkten, an denen Finanzinstrumente gehandelt werden, zuständigen Stellen der anderen Mitgliedstaaten der Europäischen Union und der anderen Vertragsstaaten des Abkommens über den Europäischen Wirtschaftsraum".

6.3.1. The German system and Basel II: *parturiunt montes* (the mountains give birth to a mouse)[156]

In the area of international cooperation, reference should be made to the recent reform of the financial system under the new Basel agreement. As previously mentioned, this agreement seeks to extend the process of harmonisation and integration of supervisory principles, in particular the principle of cooperation between the bodies charged with supervision. BaFin, which also participated in the drafting of the Basel principles, agreed to implement the accords, in spite of criticism by the German press after the agreement and by the president, J. Sanio, in an interview with the daily newspaper *Handelsblatt*.[157] The greatest uncertainties concerning the effectiveness of the accords are not so much their possibly difficult application in Europe, but rather the understandable doubt about their implementation by the United States of America. Clearly the US is the main party in this agreement: "In Europa sind die neuen Kapitalregeln seit Beginn dieses Jahres offiziell in Kraft. Viele deutsche Banken machen allerdings von einer Übergangsfrist Gebrauch und wenden Basel II erst ab dem kommenden jahr tatsächlich an. In den USA streiten Banken und Aufseher dagegen noch über die Einführung. Auf grund der unklaren Gemengelage wurden die Konsultationsphase für das Regelwerk kürzlich um zwei Monate auf Ende März 2007 verlängert. Im günstigsen Fall würden die USA Basel II nach derzeitigem Diskussionsstand sukzessive in den Jahren 2008 und 2009 einführen, also ein Jahr später als in Europa".[158] In Europe the new regulations are officially in force, while in the United States their enforceability has been challenged by the banks; there is debate about the introduction of these standards in 2008 and 2009, at least a year later than in Europe. Journalistic tone aside, Germany implemented the principles through enactment of primary and secondary legislation. Particularly worthy of mention is the *Kreditwesengesetz-KWG* amendment made by the legislative provision of 17 November 2006. It provides for a series of modifications relating to the requisites for appraising

156 ...Nascetur ridiculus mus. This is the opinion of the German journalists on the follow up of Basel II. See, amongst the others, O. Stock, *Anachronismus Basel II*, in a report pulbished on 28 June 2004 and now available on www.handelsblatt.com/News/Journal/Kommentar/_pv/grid_id/504/_p/204051/_t/ft/_b/754694/default.aspx/kommentar-anachronismus-basel-ii.html: "Lange hat der Berg gekreißt. Am Ende hat er tatsächlich mehr als eine Maus geboren. Die neuen Regeln aus Basel werden das Risikomanagement stärken und das Bonitätsdenken in Banken und Unternehmen stützen. [...] Viel entscheidender als ausgeklügelte Systeme zur Eigenkapitalunterlegung ist jedoch die Fähigkeit der Banken, Gewinne zu machen und Risiken so einzuschätzen, dass sie auch in der Krise noch flüssig bleiben. Dazu bedarf es einer verantwortungsbewussten Unternehmensführung. So etwas lässt sich erreichen, wenn den Marktteilnehmern tiefe Einblicke ins Management gewährt werden. Sie müssen in der Lage sein, die bessere Bank der schlechteren vorzuziehen. Mehr Transparenz müsste deswegen der Hauptansatz heißen – eine Forderung, die wohl Basel III vorbehalten bleibt.

157 F.M. Drost, C. Potthoff, Bafin-Chef Sanio sieht schwarz für Basel II, in www.handelsblatt.com/News/Unternehmen/Bankenversicherungen/_pv/_p/200039/_t/ft/_b/1210342/default.aspx/bafin-chef-sanio-siehtschwarz-fuer-basel-ii.html, consulted in November 2006.

158 Idem.

capital adequacy, the solidity of groups of institutions and of parent companies, to the specification of the matters subject to audit, and to the inspectional powers of BaFin.[159]

6.3.2. Cooperation between national supervisory authorities

The forms of cooperation between national authorities include the agreements between BaFin, the German Federal Bank and the Federal Cartel Authority (Federal Competition Authority), as well as the need for exchange of information, including personal data, required in order to correctly fulfil supervisory duties.[160]

Furthermore, still within the scope of national cooperation duties, there are historical ties between BaFin and the *Bundesbank*, whose involvement in the banking supervisory system is not only due to its development over time, but also to the nature of its duties. Although its objectives and tasks as Central Bank are not exactly the same as those of banking supervisors generally, the objectives and activities of monetary policy and prudential supervision often overlap or complement each other in the financial sector.

This feature causes a particular kind of similarity – and sometimes an overlapping – of functions as regards the powers that should have been transferred to the central European system from 1 January 1999.[161] The Banking Act of 1961 assigned to the Federal Banking Supervisory Office responsibility for supervision of credit institutions and – with the coming into force of the Sixth Amendment of the Banking Act – also of financial institutions.

The Federal Banking Supervisory Office took on the role of independent federal authority on 1 January 1962, charged with reporting to the Federal Ministry of Economy (and until the end of 1972, to the Federal Ministry of Finance). With the entry into force of the law on integrated supervision of financial services of 1 May 2002, the three different Federal Supervisory Offices responsible for oversight of banking, of insurance, and of securities trading were unified within a single authority assigned to supervision of the financial sector.

Because of its relations with credit institutions, its local presence and in general its proximity to market operations, the *Bundesbank* has always exercised considerable influence on the finance sector. It is no coincidence, in fact, that Section VII of the Banking Act provides for the involvement of the *Bundesbank* in banking supervision operations. *Deutsche Bundesbank* and BaFin still operate in concert today, according to their respective duties and functions, as specified by parliamentary act of agreement.[162]

159 Q3/2007, *3rd Quarter Edition* 2007, www.bafin.de/bafinjournal/bq0703_en.pdf, consulted in November 2005.

160 §6 (2) Wertpapierhandelgesetz – WpHG *cit.* states: "(2) Die Bundesanstalt, die Deutsche Bundesbank im Rahmen ihrer Tätigkeit nach Maßgabe des Kreditwesengesetzes sowie das Bundeskartellamt und die Börsenaufsichtsbehörden haben einander Beobachtungen und Feststellungen einschließlich personenbezogener Daten mitzuteilen, die für die Erfüllung ihrer Aufgaben erforderlich sind".

161 *See the opinion of the European Central Bank in* www.ecb.int/ecb/legal/pdf/en_con_2007_32_f_sign.pdf. B. Szego, *Verso un sistema bancario e finanziario europeo? La definizione di attività bancaria e finanziaria tra legge e innovazione*, in *Quaderni Ricerche*, n. 43, cur. by the *Ente per gli studi monetari bancari e finanziari Luigi Einaudi*, 1999, 10.

162 Www.bancaditalia.it/pubblicazioni/relann/rel05/rel05it/rel05_indice.pdf.

According to this agreement, most of the functions concerned with banking supervision are assigned to the *Bundesbank* because of its decades-long experience of supervisory activity in the financial market and payment operations sectors. In its activity of monitoring financial operations, it performs, among others, the functions of assessing the documentation and reports prepared annually by credit institutions.

BaFin, on the other hand, as successor to the Federal Banking Supervisory Office carries out a more secondary role in the banking sector: it is responsible for supervision of all measures of a financial nature (sovereign measures). Only in exceptional cases does it review audits of banking operations, on its own or together with the *Bundesbank*. Aside from the above mentioned supervision of credit institutions, the *Bundesbank* exercises a linking role because of its functions as Central Bank, in this way contributing to the stability of the financial system, in line with the provisions of the European System of Central Banks (ESCB). It performs important functions in: determination of general rules; supervision of banking operations, except for sovereign operations which, as previously explained, are the responsibility of BaFin; in prudential oversight of audits; and in the operations of cooperation and coordination in the sector of prudential supervision.

However BaFin's duties are not limited to performing sovereign functions, that is to say those operations authorising, monitoring and, if necessary, terminating the activity of credit institutions. They also extend to laying down guidelines of a general nature, which may consist of codes of conduct that the banks are obliged to follow, and rules about new financial services or services that hold risks. In addition its functions may also involve resolving problems related to banking and financial services, when they endanger the stability of institutional structures or when in some way they may jeopardise the economic system as a whole.

Also in the area of authority powers, there exists a duty of mutual cooperation between BaFin and the *Bundesbank*. This cooperation takes the form of the *Bundesbank*'s participation in enactment of secondary legislation, in bank inspections, in international cooperation and coordination, and in the management of any crises in the sector.

With specific regard to cooperation in ongoing supervision of credit institutions, the law reforming supervisory authorities provides that BaFin is responsible for adopting administrative measures on the basis of the results of controls and of further monitoring carried out by the *Bundesbank*, which in turn acts in compliance with the guidelines issued by BaFin.

In extremely simplified terms, it may be said that ongoing supervision, generally carried by peripheral units of the *Bundesbank*, consists in: analysis of reports provided by credit institutions, of audit reports, and of documents related to annual accounts; carrying out and analysing the results of technical bank monitoring with the objective of judging the adequacy of capital reserves and of risk management procedures; and assessing the results of investigations.

In the area of inspectional supervision, the auditing companies play an important role: they draft detailed annual reports on the overall situation of intermediaries, and are also obliged to immediately inform BaFin if they discover evident irregularities in the financial system.

Moreover, BaFin may carry out extraordinary sector inspections; these are generally delegated to auditing companies or to the *Bundesbank*.[163]

7. *Regulatory supervision and internal audits*

The KWG regulates in detail the activities of credit institutions, in the area of regulatory supervision, causing significant reduction in the margins of discretionary power that the supervisory authority had in performing its activity.

The main competencies of BaFin as regards secondary legislation are clarification of prudential rules concerning capital adequacy and liquidity, as well as defining best practice in the internal organisation of the institutions which it oversees. As regards adequate capital resources of intermediaries, this is defined by the KWG. Further regulation is referred to BaFin, whose autonomy is limited on one hand by the provisions contained in the European directives, and on the other by the binding opinions of the *Bundesbank*.

Regulations on specific organisational duties for credit institutions were introduced by the sixth amendment to the KWG, in order to extend the possibilities of intervention on the part of authorities overseeing bank organisation. Article 25a, subsection 1, confirms the obligation of credit institutions to provide themselves with an adequate risk management system, with a well-organised structure, with an adequate control system, and with good information systems security.[164]

Risk management has also been recently regulated through development of best practices that provide minimum standards for administration of the credit area and the credit process (*Mindestanforderungen an das Kreditgeschäft* - MAK).[165] BaFin's purpose, in defining these practices, is to reinforce awareness of risks adopted by banks and to improve transparency.[166]

163 Gesetz über den Wertpapierhandel, WpHG *cit.*, Part. II, Sect. IV, §3: "Die Bundesanstalt kann von jedermann Auskünfte, die Vorlage von Unterlagen und die Überlassung von Kopien verlangen sowie Personen laden und vernehmen, soweit dies auf Grund von Anhaltspunkten für die Überwachung der Einhaltung eines Verbots oder Gebots dieses Gesetzes erforderlich ist. Sie kann insbesondere die Angabe von Bestandsveränderungen in Finanzinstrumenten sowie Auskünfte über die Identität weiterer Personen, insbesondere der Auftraggeber und der aus Geschäften berechtigten oder verpflichteten Personen, verlangen. Gesetzliche Auskunfts- oder Aussageverweigerungsrechte sowie gesetzliche Verschwiegenheitspflichten bleiben unberührt".

164 BAKred, *Jahresbericht 2000*, 2001, 12 and ff.

165 BaFin, 2002d, in www.bafin.de.

166 Paragraph 7, Sect. 37 b WpGH 9 September 1998 *cit.*: "Unterlässt es der Emittent von Finanzinstrumenten, die zum Handel an einer inländischen Börse zugelassen sind, unverzüglich eine neue Tatsache zu veröffentlichen, die ihn unmittelbar betrifft, ist er einem Dritten zum Ersatz des durch die Unterlassung entstandenen Schadens verpflichtet, wenn der Dritte: 1. die Finanzinstrumente nach der Unterlassung erwirbt und er bei Bekanntwerden der Insiderinformation noch Inhaber der Finanzinstrumente ist oder; 2. die Finanzinstrumente vor dem Entstehen der Insiderinformation erwirbt und nach der Unterlassung veräußert".

The MAKs made definition of a credit risk strategy compulsory, as well as separation of operating functions from control functions, definition of the entire credit process, and monitoring of possible related risks.

8. *Concluding comment*

In the Federal Republic of Germany, traditionally characterised by a large number of banks, a low degree of concentration, and a strong public sector presence, regulatory policies have never aimed to have much effect on the structure of the banking system.

Therefore, among all the German supervisory authorities, there is no body that carries out a real function as leader in the banking system.

On this point, it has been stated that "BaFin's lack of independence from political power, counterbalanced by the *Bundesbank*'s involvement in supervision, and consequent incomplete autonomy in carrying out supervision, seem to constitute important limitations to the institution's capacity to act as the primary external interlocutor and central reference point of the whole banking system".[167]

The absence of new ambitions in terms of legislation, aimed at promoting increasing regulation of the market, shifts attention towards the external pressure of Community sources, currently viewed as one of the most effective factors stimulating modernisation of the entire system: "Since the 1990s, European harmonisation has increasingly driven changes in banking regulation. The adoption of EU regulation required extensive amendments to the banking act. One important example is the adoption of the own funds directive and the capital adequacy directive [...], which led to a substantial increase in capital requirements for banks. Notwithstanding such adjustments, the amendments left the supervisory concept embedded in the banking act – imposing exposure limits relative to banks capital – intact".[168]

Section 2. Liability

1. *On public administration liability in general*

In the Federal Republic of Germany, the system of State liability (*Staatshaftungsrecht*) is not grounded on a single regulatory structure; public administration liability is regulated through case law, which has built up through the application of positive law and which

167 C. Di Capua, *Il sistema bancario tedesco cit.*, 118: "la mancanza di indipendenza dal potere politico della Bafin, controbilanciata dalla partecipazione della Bundesbank alla vigilanza, e la conseguente incompleta autonomia nello svolgimento della funzione di vigilanza sembrano rappresentare limiti non secondari per la capacità dell'ente di proporsi come interlocutore esterno primario e punto di riferimento centrale di tutto il sistema bancario".

168 D. Domanski, *The impact of financial regulation on financial structures in post-war Germany*, in *Quaderni di Ricerche realizzati nell'ambito della ricerca "Verso un sistema bancario e finanziario europeo"*, a cura dell'Ente per gli Studi Monetari, Bancari e Finanziari *Luigi Einaudi*, n. 45, 2003, 10.

has relatively few regulations, fundamentally the provisions in §839 of BGB and article 34 GG.[169]

In particular, §839 BGB provides for the situation in which an official violates an official duty towards a third party wilfully or with gross negligence. In this case, he is obliged to provide compensation for any damage caused only if the injured party is not able to obtain compensation in any other way.[170] The second subsection of the above section also extends the application of these rules to officials responsible for issuing decisions on a legal dispute. The third subsection specifies that this provision does not apply in cases in which the injured party negligently or wilfully failed to prevent the damage, not performing any specific remedy otherwise provided for by the law.

Article 34 GG provides that when a public official breaches an official duty that he holds towards a third party, the State or the public body for which he works is liable. Any action of recourse for offences committed wilfully or with gross negligence can be made in a civil court, as can damages claims.

In identifying possible situations of public administration liability in the German system, it is first necessary to take account of all cases of occurrence of *Haftung für höhleitliches Unrecht*, that is to say, liability for breaching norms which regulate the activity of those in authority. In this respect, distinction is made between:

a) *Amtshaftung* claims, based on the combined provisions of §839 BGB and Article 34 GG. As already mentioned, in order to combine these, there must be no grounds excluding and/or limiting liability (§839, I, 2 BGB *cit.*, the so-called *Mitverschulden*, or presumption of *Versäumung der Rechtsmittel*, provided for by §839 *cit.*). Such cases, to which the general time limits for damages claims apply (three years), must be heard by a civil judge, against the public administration, which may also bring a separate claim against the public official.[171]
b) *Aufopferung* (literally "sacrifice") claims; this type of claim is made in the event of alleged breach of any fundamental right, under Article 2 II GG. Such claims may be brought in any cases in which there has been unlawful intrusion by state authorities in the legal sphere of a private individual, causing damage to him or her.[172]
c) Claims for protection in cases of damage to property suffered as a result of unlawful removal on the part of the public administration, similar to expropriation ("*Der*

[169] F. Ossenbühl, *Staatshaftungsrecht*, München, V ed., 1998; K. Windhorst, H.D. Sproll, S. Detterbeck, *Staatshaftungsrecht*, München, 2000; B. Bender, *Staatshaftungsrecht*, Heidelberg, 1981; M. Carrà, *Risarcimento in forma specifica e* Folgenbeseitigung, in *Dir. amm.*, 2004, 799.

[170] S. Detterbeck, *Allgemeines Verwaltungsrecht*, München, 2002, 309; H. Maurer, *Allgemeines verwaltungsrecht*, München, 2004, §§25 and ff.; F. Schoch, *Amtshaftung*, in *Jura*, 1988, 585.

[171] H. Stoll, *Il risarcimento del danno nel diritto tedesco*, in S. Patti (ed.), *Annuario di diritto tedesco*, 2001, Milano, 169; A. Colombi Ciacchi, *Alla ricerca della determinatezza della fattispecie colposa: i recenti sviluppi della dottrina tedesca*, *ivi*, 2004, 499.

[172] O. Mayer, *Die Haftung des Staates für rechtswidrige Amtshandlungen*, in *Sächsisches Archiv für Rechtspflege*, 1913, 11, and furthermore in the three editions of the II volume of *Deutsches Verwaltungsrecht*, 1896 (p. 345 and ff.), 1917 (p. 516 and ff.) and 1924 (p. 295 and ff.); see also W. Schmidt, *Die Aufopferung vermögenswerter Rechte*, *NJW*, 1999, 2847.

Anspruch wegen rechtswidriger Eigentumsverletzung – enteignungsleicher Eingriff")[173];

d) Claims for termination of execution and performance and for elimination of consequences arising from unlawful action of the public administration, upon annulment or withdrawal of the order (*Folgenbeseitigungsanspruch* means literally: removal of consequences).

Naturally, more than one of these cases listed may occur together. Generally, nearly all of them may be brought alongside an *Amtshaftung* claim. For example, regarding the relationship between this type of claim and the action taken in the case of expropriation for public use, the law has established that it does not conform either with the specialty principle or with the subsidiarity principle, since the rulings they relate to have different characteristics.

The situation is different when it is possible to resort to restitutive remedies under d), where the general preclusive principle of the so-called "priority of the primary norm" (*Vorrang des primarrechtsschutzes*) finds application; it operates when determining relationships between the application of constitutive remedies (aimed at removing public administration invalidity) and the actuation of compensatory remedies in the broad sense.[174]

This approach does not seem to be unanimously shared by judiciary, in the sense that failure to resort to jurisdictional protection is often interpreted in terms of contributory negligence, so that the civil judge has to deal with the question of the legitimacy of the act. The most obvious case is that of liability for breach of official duties. The third subsection of §839 of the BGB, as seen above, specifically stipulates that no compensatory obligation exists ("*Die Ersatzplicht tritt nicht ein*") if the injured party negligently or wilfully has failed to perform a specific remedy.

2. *Liability of supervisory bodies*

Liability of supervisory bodies for non-fulfilment of the duties assigned to them is very frequently based on provisions relating to unlawful conduct of public employees and officials, particularly for those bodies charged with oversight of the so-called sensitive areas.

173 H. Maurer, *Allgemeines Verwaltungsrecht cit.*, 709 and ff.

174 BVerfGE, 15 July 1981, in *BVerfGE* 58, 300. See W. Rüfner, *Basic Elements of German Law on State Liability*, in J. Bell and A.W. Bradley, *Governmental Liability: a Comparative Study*, UKNNCL, 1991, 248, 260: "the consequences of this decision are as yet unclear. Initially some writers maintained that the entire concept developed under the notion of 'quasi-espropriatory enchroachment' should be abandoned. Later the view prevailed that the further development of the law on state liability could not simply be discontinued. In particular, the failure of the State Liability Act, which put off a possible reform to a remote future, made it impossible to imagine that one could go solely on the restricted basis of a fault related claim in tortious governmental liability".

As previously stated, according to Article 34 GG, the administration is liable in all those cases in which a breach has occurred of official duties towards a third party.[175]

As experts have pointed out, the notion of *Drittbezogenheit*, or breach of official duty, is central to issues regarding public administration liability.[176]

In this regard, there is justification for coordination of provisions contained in Article 34 GG with those in §839 BGB, confirming the liability of public employees who, during the performance of the duties assigned to them, cause damage to a third party.[177]

Once a "reflected" liability of the State for an action carried out by an employee in performing official duties has been established that the crucial issue is the need to identify those who are able to initiate legal proceedings in order to obtain remedy for harm suffered as a consequence of the public administration's unlawful conduct.

It has been pointed out that, in the case of action taken by the body regulating the stock market, essentially aimed at safeguarding the public interest, a single individual was not granted the right to take legal action in order to protect his or her personal legal situation because the regulatory body's action was not directed at him or her.[178]

In the same way, in the area of finance, and especially in the credit and insurance sectors, German law long remained anchored to the idea that powers conferred by sector regulations on the supervisory authorities were aimed at the protection of the public

175 Art. 34 GG states: "*Verletz jemand in Ausübung eines ihm anvertrauten öffentlichen Amtes die ihm einem Dritten gegenüber obliegende Amtspflicht, so trifft die Verantwortlichkeit grundsatzlich den Staat oder die Körperschaft, in deren Dienst er steht*".

176 M. Clarich, *La responsabilità della Consob nell'esercizio della funzione di vigilanza: due passi oltre la sentenza della Corte di cassazione n. 500/99*, in *Danno e resp.*, 2002, 346.

177 J. Hecker, *sub §839 BGB*, in *Erman BGB 11. Auflage. Band II*, herausgegeben von H. P. Westermann, Köln, 2004, 3132: "Art. 34 GG enthält selbst keine erschöpfende Regelung der Amtshaftung, sondern staetz ein Verhalten voraus, das den Tatbestand des §839 erfüllt". "Die Haftungsügernahme wird ferner nur 'grundsätzlich' angeordnet; dies läßt Raum für sondergesetzliche Haftungsausschulüsse und – beschränkungen"). "Als bloße Zurechnungsnorm verlargert Art. 34 GG die Haftung auf den Verwaltungsträger, der Anstelle und nicht neben dem Beamten haftet. Im Grundsatz haftet der Staat daher nur im gleichen Umfang, wie der Amtsträger selbst es müßte, wenn es die Schuldübernahme nicht gäbe; die auf die persönliche Verantwortlichkeit des Amsträgers zugeschnittenen gesetzlichen Haftungsbeschränkungen, – milderungen oder – privilegien kommen daher mittelbar auch dem Staat zugute". According to the Author the two provisions are not perfectly coordinated: "Beide Normen sind jedoch nocht deckungsgleich. Art. GG nimmt den privatrechtlichen Funktionskreis von der Haftunsübernahme". See also Mahendra P. Singh, *German Administrative Law in Common Law Perspective*, Heidelberg, 2001, 257 "this part of the German law corresponds to the distinction which the French law draws between the faute personnelle and the faute de service and the English law draws between the acts in the course of employment and those not in course of employment. In the French law the distinction between the faute personnelle and the faute de service has led to the evolution of the principle of cumul which creates wider scope for the victim of tort to recover damages from the state. The German law has not evolved to that extent and remains closer to the common law in this respect. However, the German courts have given up a narrow or restrictive approach to the interpretation of the exercise of public authority and would like to enable the individual to recover damages from the state".

178 B.S. Markesinis, *The German Law of Obligations*, vol. II, *The Law of Torts: A Comparative Introduction*, Oxford, 1997, 904: "the State's activity cannot be engaged if the requirements of §839 BGB are not satisfied. Looking at them, however, one sees clear signs of a protective philosophy which may have made sense at the turn of the century but which nowadays appears less convincing".

interest, thus excluding the possibility that the authorities could be held liable towards a third party.

A complete change of judicial attitude occurred in 1979, when the Federal Administrative Tribunal, in two bank failure cases (*Wetterstein* and *Herstatt*[179]), ordered that investors in a banking institution, who had suffered damage as a consequence of lack of supervision on the part of the Federal Office for Banking Supervision (*Bundessaufsuchstamt für das Kreditwesen*), were entitled to take legal action in order to obtain compensation for the losses arising from breach of the Office's duty to protect.[180]

Pronouncement of the liability of the credit supervisory authority was based on a strict interpretation of the 1961 Banking Law (*Kreditwesengesetz*), that enabled direct protection of investors considered as single users to be identified as one of the various aims of the law, and established the same law as a default rule for all cases not already provided for in a different manner under specific sector regulations.

The sudden increase in supervisory authority liability had such a disruptive effect within the German credit system that, in order to avoid the possibility of an overload in legal disputes which would have been difficult to manage, §6 of the KWG was amended in 1984. This restored the original concept according to which all duties performed by supervisory authorities were exclusively aimed at protecting the public interest.[181]

With this surprising backlash, the ability of investors to take legal action for liability against supervisory authorities was definitively repressed. Still today, only banks can start proceedings for liability under §839 BGB and 34 GG, in cases in which they are the direct addressees of activity carried out by the supervisory body, and not in all cases where this activity is generally addressed towards the pursuit of the public interest.[182]

3. *The German system of supervision and Community law*

The difficulties concerning the German prudential supervisory system have been recently addressed with the ruling of the European Court of Justice of 12 October 2004, case C-

179 See BGH, 15 February 1979, in *NJW*, 1979, 1354 e BGH, 12 July 1979, *ibidem*, 1879. M. Tison, *Challenging the Prudential Supervisor: Liability* versus *Regulatory Immunity, Paper prepared for the SUERF Conference "stability and efficiency of financial market in Central and Eastern Europe"*, Tallinn, 12–14 June 2003, 9.

180 A. Seban, *Le juge administratif doit-il retenir une faute lorde ou une faute simple pour engager le responsabilité de l'Etat à raison de la surveillance exercée par la Commission bancaire sur les établissements de crédit?*, in *Conclusions sous Conseil d'Etat, Assemblée 30 novembre 2001, n. 219562, Ministre de l'Economie et des finances c/ M. Kenichchian et autres, on line www.rajf.org*, consulted in March 2007.

181 J. Horn, *"Germany"*, in *Banking Supervision in the European Community. Institutional Aspects*, Brussels, *Edition de l'ULB*, 1995, 142. M. Tison, *Challenging the Prudential Supervisor cit.*, 11 who states that the main objective of the provision is "to fend off liability claims in the future, by indicating that prudential supervision did not serve the protection of individual creditors.

182 P. Ulmer, *Sub §839 BGB*, in Münchener Kommentar – Bürgerliches Gesetzbuch – Schuldrecht – Besonderer Teil III, K. Rebmann – F.J. Säcker – R. Rixecker, München, 2004.

222/02.[183] The preliminary question, submitted to the Court of Justice in the case under consideration, related to the relationship between the German national legal system and directives on prudential supervision (particularly their relationship with Article 839 of the *Bürgerliches Gesetzbuch*, the German civil code, and with Article 6 of the *Gesetz ber das Kreditwesen*, or Credit Law). It was raised by the *Bundesgerichtshof* (German Court of Cassation) in a civil case brought by a private citizen who suffered damage as a result of the failure of a bank in which he had deposited his savings; he decided to sue the *Bundesrepublik Deutschland* in order to recover compensation for the damage he sustained due to the German State's failure to implement Directive 94/19/CE on the deposit guarantee system.

The claimant argued that if the German State had implemented Directive 94/19/CE within the time limit specified (1 July 1995), the bank holding his savings would have had its authorisation to operate as a credit institution withdrawn well before it failed.

The directive confers on the *Bundesaufsichtsamt für das Kreditwesen* (Federal Office of Credit Institute Supervision) the task of adopting appropriate measures towards the credit institutions which do not comply with the obligation to be part of a deposit guarantee system, thus devolving to the above regulator the authority to adopt the necessary measures.

In this specific case, between 1991 and 1997 the claimant had made considerable deposits with the bank, which then failed, while the above directive, including the powers conferred on the *Bundesaufsichtsamt für das Kreditwesen*, only became part of the German legal system in August 1998.

The belated implementation of this directive, therefore, appeared to have impeded the introduction, on the part of the regulator responsible, of the necessary deposit protection measures.

During the final appeal, the *Bundesgerichtshof* asked the European Court of Justice to verify compatibility with Directives 77/780, 89/299, 89/646, and 94/19, of Article 839 of the *Bürgerliches Gesetzbuch*, which declares that: "the public official who, wilfully or with gross negligence, violates the obligations of his office toward a third party must compensate the third party for the damage arising from his actions"; of Article 34 of the *Grundgesetz* (Fundamental law), according to which "if a public official, in performing his functions, violates the obligations imposed by his office towards a third party, liability rests primarily with the State or with the institution where the official is employed"; and especially of Article 6, no. 4, of the *Gesetz über das Kreditwesen* (Law on Credit), which stipulates that "the *Bundesaufsichtsamt* carries out the tasks assigned to it by this law and by other laws exclusively in the public interest".

The court ruled that both Directive 94/19/CE, and the "system" arising from the combined dispositions of the directives mentioned above are not in contrast with the

[183] See comments in *NJW*, 2004, 3479, in *Common Market Law Review*, 2005 f. 3, note by M. Tison, *Do not attack the watchdog! Banking supervisor's liability after Peter Paul*, in *Giur. it.*, 2005, 390, note by D. Siclari, Drittbezogenheit *del dovere d'ufficio*, öffentlichen Interesse *ed esclusione della responsabilità dell'autorità di vigilanza bancaria nell'ordinamento tedesco*, in *Foro it.*, 2005, IV, 101, in *Riv. it. dir. pubbl. com.*, 2005, f. 3-4, note by M. Poto, *La Corte di Giustizia ed il sistema tedesco di vigilanza prudenziale: la* primauté *si scontra con il vecchio adagio* ubi maior, minor cessat.

national disposition according to which supervision of credit institutions is carried out only in the public interest. This, therefore, means that national dispositions that exclude individuals from recovering compensation for damage caused by deficient supervision on the part of the relevant sector authority are compatible with Community law.

Two main points emerge thus far which the Court particularly emphasises: on the one hand, the fact that directives on supervision may not be interpreted in such a way as to confer on investors further rights compared to those guaranteed by the national legal system, in the event of unavailability of their deposits, with inadequate supervision on the part of the competent national authority. On the other hand, and as a direct consequence of such a conclusion, it is expressly stated that Directives 77/780, 89/299 and 89/646 are not in contrast with national law according to which the duties of the national supervisory authority as regards credit institutions are exclusively performed in the public interest, thus excluding individuals from the possibility of seeking compensation for damage caused by inadequate supervision on the part of this supervisory authority.

The issues dealt with by the Community judges are, therefore, of indisputable importance in terms of the relationship between national legislation and Community legislation. Although they are formally irreproachable in terms of correct application of Community principles concerning State liability for failure to implement directives, they nevertheless appear to raise some questions regarding correct application of the effective guarantee principle, at least as regards its practical repercussions on and its concrete applicability to legal situations involving addressees of the norms on supervision.

4. *The influence of Community law on Bundesgerichtshof decisions*

The ruling of the European Court of Justice constitutes one of the central points around which the reasoning of a recent decision by the *Bundesgerichtshof* was constructed; this related to rejection of a damages claim made by a group of deposit-holders against BaFin for negligent supervision. The investigation into the legitimacy of the compensation claim by the aggrieved clients carried out by the German Supreme Court focused on analysis of the combined dispositions of §6, par. IV of the KWG and of §4, par. IV of the FinDAG and its compatibility with Community law on the one hand, and with national legislation on the other.[184]

The damages claim had been made by a group of clients of the BVH-Bank, who, following a series of heavy losses in their deposits with this bank, initiated legal action against the Federal Republic of Germany; they claimed the direct involvement, and therefore liability for losses, of the credit supervisory Authority for negligent oversight of administration of banking operations.[185]

184 V. BGH, urteil vom 20.1.2005, III ZR 48/01 (OLG Köln), in *NJW*, 2005, 11.

185 The judgement incipit states: "Die Kl. Haben ihren Schaden darauf zurückgeführt, dass das Bundesaufsichtsamt (the Supervisory Authority) seinen Aufsichtsplichten nicht hinreichend nachgekommen sei (was negliglent in its supervisory tasks) und nicht zu einem früheren Zeitpunkt Maßnahmen nach §§6 III, 33, 45, 46 KWG ergriffen habe" (and has not taken decisions according to §§6, III, 33, 45, 46 KWG).

On the other side, the defending *Bundesrepublik* based its defence on the argument that single individuals have no right to sue, since duty of care is to be performed solely for the protection of the public interest: "das Amt nehme seine Aufgaben nur in öffentlichen Interesse war".

Furthermore, in the well-constructed presentation of its defence, the Federal Republic asserted the lack of grounds for all damages claims against the State for non-compliance with Community duties, or *Staatshaftungsanspruchs* (also referring to the ruling of the European Court of Justice of 12 October 2004 c-222/02), as well as the groundlessness of the claimant's case based on the alleged breach of official duties on the part of the supervisory Authority (*Amtsshaftungsgrundssätzen*).

In relation to the first point, the *Bundesrepublik* argument makes reference to the decision of the European Court of Justice, according to which three requirements must be fulfilled before the State can be held legally responsible for non-compliance with Community directives, and therefore before an individual's damages claim can be considered legitimate:

1) the regulation which is considered to have been breached must specifically recognise the status of individuals;
2) the unlawful conduct must consist in violation of that regulation;
3) the existence of a causal relationship between the unlawful conduct and the damage claimed must be proved.[186]

The reasoning of the *Bundesrepublik* is founded specifically on the basis of the established non-existence of an explicit provision of this kind in Community legislation, confirmed by the European Court of Justice's ruling which, as already mentioned, in the ruling of 12 October 2004 rejected the possibility of interpreting directives concerning supervision as directly awarding rights to deposit-holders, in the event of unavailability of their deposits, when claiming negligent supervision on the part of the national supervisory authority.

From this, the *Bundesrepublik* argued that the supervisory authority acts for a purpose which may only be considered as being aimed at the protection of public interest: "auch soweit aufsichtrechtlich relevante Richtlinien keinen ausdrücklichen Hinweis (in

[186] See §I.1 judgm. *cit.*: "Nach dem vom EuGH entiwickelten gemeinschaftsrechtlichen Staatshaftungsanspruch für Versöße der Mitgliedstaaten gegen das Gemeinshaftsrecht kommt eine Haftung des Mitgliedstaats dann in Betracht wenn die verlezte Gemeinschaftsrechtsnorm bezweckt, dem Einzelnen Rechte zu verleihen, der Verstoß hinreichend qualifiziert ist und zwischen diesem Verstoß und dem dem Einzelnen entstandenen Schaden ein unmittelbarer Kausalzusammenhang besteht". On the relationship between EU Law and German law, see F. Mayer, *The European Constitution and the Courts. Adjudicating European constitutional law in a multilevel system*, Heidelberg, 24–27 February 2003, Jean Monnet Working paper, no. 9, 2003. More in general on the compliance with the EU law see W. Van Gerven, *The ECJ's recent case-law in the field of Tort Liability, towards a European* Ius Commune and M. Fierstra, *The Significance of the Francovich Jurisprudence for the National Courts*; G. Krohn, *Government Liability in Germany for Infringement of Community Law*, published in R.H.M. Jansen, D.A.C. Koster, R.F.B. Van Zutphen, *European Ambitions of National Judiciary*, The Hague, 1998, 91, 111, 119.

the directives no explicit mention is found) auf den Anlegerschutz enthielten (for the protection of investors), seien sie Teil eines bankenaufsichtechtlichen Gesamtregelungswerks, das in seiner praktischen Wirksamkeit ausgehöhlt würde, wenn die Aufsichtbehörden ihre Tätigkeit nur in öffentlichen Interesse wahrnähmen".

The second point on which the defence of the *Bundesrepublik* is based concerns analysis of the difficulties connected with a possible "system fault", an analysis which, in the opinion of the Federal Republic of Germany, can only result in the demonstrated non-existence of any possible liability. For this to exist, the claimant would have to prove the actual existence of a regulation recognising that their legal position was entitled to protection: an *Interesse* that is not, however, *öffentliche*, but rather purpose-oriented ("*nach dem Zweck*"): "vielmehr ist jeweils zu prüfen, ob gerade das in Einzelfall berührte Interesse nach dem Zweck und der recthlicjen Bestimmung des Amtsgeschäfts geschützt werden soll".[187]

Indicating the content of Parliamentary proceedings concerning the approval of the 1984 financial law (KWG of 20.12.1984)[188] and also the interpretation made by the *Bundesgerichtshof*[189], the defending public administration referred to their interpretation of §6, par. III KWG, according to which the supervisory authority, in fulfilling its official duties that include, along with other activities, supervision over the transparency and correctness of accounts ("*Verstandnis von der Zielrichtung der Staatlichen Bankausicht*"), acts in the public interest (point 2, paragraph I).

The above defence of the public administration was accepted by the BGH, and consequently the damages claim advanced by the deposit-holders was rejected: "so dass auch §6 IV KWG einer Haftung nicht entgegenstünde, kommt eine Schadensersatzplich der Bekl. (of the defending party) nicht in Bertracht".[190]

5. *Concluding comment*

To sum up, the law regarding the liability of supervisory authorities in the German system seems to be based on the use of a well-defined criterion that distinguishes between regulations which provide for only *öffentliche Interesse* in the legitimacy of public administration activity, and regulations in which, on the contrary, interest seems to be

187 O. Mayer, *Deutsches Verwaltungsrecht*, Leipzig, 1895; V.R. Tezner, *Die Deutschen Theorien der Vewaltungsrechtsplege, Separatabdruck aus dem Verwaltungsarchiv*, Berlin, 1901; R. Von Laun, *Das Freie Ermessen und seine Grenzen*, Leipzig und Wien, 1910, in part. p. 61 and ff.; W. Horstmann, *Das öffentliche Interesse und seine Vertretung vor den Verwaltungsgerichten, Inauguraldissertation zur Erlangung der juristichen Doktorwürde der Rechts- und Staatswissenschaftlichen Fakultät der Universität zu Göttingen*, Göttingen, 1938.

188 V. Gesetzentwurf der Bundesregierung (BT-Dr 10/1441, 20): "Die Änderung stellt für sämtliche dem Bundesaufsichtamt zugewiesenen Aufgaben klar, dass sie zur Sicherstellung der Funktionsfähigkeit der Kreditwirtshaft ausschließlich im öffentliche Interesse wahrgenoomen werden [...]". See also BGH, Urteil vom 2.6.2005 III ZR 365/03, in www.recht-in.de: "Die Bankenaufsicht hat die Funktionsfähigkeit der Krediwirtschaft im öffentliche Interesse wahrzunehmen un dabei selbstverständlich die Grenzen ihrer Eingriffsbefugnisse zu beachten" (§2, II par.).

189 BGH, Urteil vom 15.2.1979, III ZR 108/76 (München), in *NJW*; Heft 27, 1354, BGH, Urteil vom 12.7.1979, III ZR 154/77 (Köln), in *NJW*; Heft 37, 1879.

190 §3 urteil BGH, 20.1.2005 *cit.*

defined according to the specific purpose that the public administration aims to pursue (*Interesse nach dem Zweck*).[191]

Precisely with reference to the relation between *Interesse nach dem Zweck* and the legal position of individuals upheld by the court, the so-called "personal" public law (*das subjective Offentliche Recht*), it is reasonable to consider the BGH's decision as an element which perfectly fits into the mosaic of the protection of the personal position of individuals in the German system.

In line on this matter with a well-consolidated jurisprudential approach, defining "personal" public law "die dem einzelnen kraft öffentlichen Rechts verliene Rechtmacht, vom Staat zur Verfolgung eineger Interessen ein bestimmtes Verhalten verlangen zu können"[192], legal scholars identify a specific connection between the individual's personal position and the need for the public authorities to behave in a certain way ("*bestimmt Verhalten*") in the pursuit of the public interest ("*zur Verfolgung eineger Interessen*").

This leads to the very clear definition of the defining features of *öffentliche Interesse*[193]: intrinsic to it is a specific objective ("*der Zweck*") which the law identifies, and which at the same time constitutes the specific objective in public action and the basis for the individual's claim regarding that action.[194]

Closely connected with such a claim, and almost inevitable consequence of it, is the legitimate expectation of the private citizen to receive protection in the event that a breach of a legal disposition should occur. Hence the statement regarding the practical aspect of "personal" public law, which is based on the possibility of jurisdictional monitoring of the same ("Die Praktische Bedeutung der subjectiven öffentlichen Rechte liegt in der Möglichkeit ihrer gerechtlichen Durchsetzbarkeit").[195]

191 BGH, Urteil vom 18.2.1999, III ZR 272/96 (Koblenz), in *NVwZ* 1999, Heft 6, 689, also in *NJW*, 1999, 2275: "Dabei genügtes, daß die Amtsplicht neben der Erfüllung allgemeiner Interessen und öffentlicher Zwecke auch den Zweck verfolgt, die Interessen einzelner wahrzunehmen" (p. 690).

192 H. Maurer, *Allgemeines Verwaltungsrecht*, München, 2004, in part. p. 163 and ff., See also G. Jellinek, *System der subjectiven öffentlichen Interesse*, Tübingen, 1919; R. Rainer, *Die doppelte Abhangigkeit des subjectiven öffentlichen Rechts*, in *Deutsches Verwaltungsblatt*, 1996, 641.

193 H. Maurer, *Allgemeines Verwaltungsrecht cit.*, in part. p. 166: "Die Verwaltung wird im öffentlichen Interesse tätig: das Verwaltungsrecht regelt die an den öffentlichen Interessen orientierte Verwaltung. Dabei geht es zwar oft – aber keineswegs immer – um die Abgrenzung öffentlicher und privater Interessen. Die Lehre vom subjektiven öffentlichen Recht knüpft daran an nach der herrschenden Schutznormtheorie liegt dann ein subjektives Recht vor, wenn eine zwingende Rechtsvorschrift (und damit die sichaus dieser Rechtsvorschrift der Verwaltung) nicht nur dem öffentlichen Interesse, sondern – zumindest auch – dem Interesse einzelner Bürger zu dienen bestimmt ist. Maßgeblich ist der gesetzlich bezweckte Interessensschutz"; see also M. Nettesheim, "*Verwaltungsrecht*", "*Vertrauensschutz*", "*Rückwirkungsverbot*", in J. Monar – N. Nowak – P. Noack (eds.), *Handwörterbuch zur Europäischen Union*, Kröner, Stuttgart 1993, 297, 358, 360.

194 G. Jellinek, *System der subjektiven öffentlichen Rechte cit.*, 68: "Das subjektive öffentliche Recht des Subjizierten wird durch das objektive Recht nicht nur geschaffen und geschützt, sondern auch realisiert".

195 H. Maurer, *Allgemeines Verwaltungsrecht cit.*, 164: "Nach Article 19 GG steht jedem, der durch die öffentlichen Gewalt in seinen subjectiven Rechten verletz ist, der Rechtsweg (= Gerichtsweg) offen. Der Bürger kann dann aber grundsätzlich auch nur dann, die Gerichte anrufen, wenn er die Verlezung 'subjective Rechte' geltend machen kann". See also Mahendra P. Singh, *German Administrative Law in Common Law Perspective*, Heidelberg, 2001, 253: "...mere insuitability (Unzweckmäßigkeit) of the decision is not enough for constituting liability. There must be a clear case of misuse of discretion amounting to its illegality".

Chapter 4

CHAPTER 4. THE BRITISH SYSTEM

Section 1. Powers

1. *On supervision of the financial system in the United Kingdom, and the decision to devolve the various market segments to a single authority*

The reform of the financial system, implemented in the UK in the four-year period between 1997 and 2001, is the basic element from which it is possible to understand the current system in the UK.[196] The reform marks the transition from a largely tripartite system, typified by the existence of three distinct market segments (deposit banks, secondary banks, and building societies and saving banks), to a unified system; this, although based on a pre-existing structure, appears to be considerably strengthened, due

196 E. Ferran, *Examining the United Kingdom's experience in adopting the single financial regulator model*, in *Brook. Journ. of International Law*, 2003, 257, in part. 265: "the history of the U.K. securities regulation in the 1980s and early 1990s paralleled that of banking regulation; it is the story of a system that was undermined by financial scandals that badly affected consumer confidence". D. Siclari, *Costituzione e autorità di vigilanza bancaria*, Padova, 2007, 70 and ff., See also R. Kinsella, *Some Regulatory and Supervisory Lessons of the BBCI Collapse*, in *Research Paper*, n. 92/10. *Research Papers in Banking and Finance*, Dublin, 1992; ID., *Regulation, Corporate Governance and Ethics in Financial Services*, London, 2005; ID., *The development of a European Central Banking System: Some Issues*, in R. Kinsella, *New Issues in Financial Services*, Blackwell, Oxford, 1992, 212. P. Truell and L. Gurwin, *False Profits: The Inside Story of BBCI, The World's most corrupt financial Empire*, 1992. On the financial crisis see A.C. Fawcett, *Examining the Objectives of Financial Regulation - Will the New Regime Succeed? A Practitioner's View*, in E. Ferran, C.A.E. Goodhart, *Regulating Financial Services and Markets in the Twenty First Century*, Cambridge, 2001, 37. C. Gola e A. Rosselli, *Il sistema bancario del Regno Unito e la riforma della vigilanza*, in *Quaderni di ricerche*, 42, *Ente per gli studi monetari e finanziari Luigi Einaudi*, 1999; F. Rossi, *Tort Liability of Financial Regulators. A comparative Study of Italian and English Law in a European Context*, *EBLR*, 2002, 643; J.R. Adams, D. Frantz, *A full Service Bank*, Simon & Schuster, 1992, A. Bowen, G. Hoggart, D. Pain, *The recent evolution of the UK banking industry and some implications for financial stability*, *BRI*, 1999; M. Taylor, *Accountability and objectives of the FSA*, in M. Blair (ed.), *Blackstone's Guide to the Financial Services and Markets Act 2000*, Blackstone Press. C. Di Noia, L. Piatti, *Regolamentazione e mercato finanziario: analisi e prospettive di riforma per il sistema italiano*, in *Consob Quaderni di Finanza*, n. 30, 1998, 1 6.

to the devolution of supervisory functions to a single body, the Financial Services Authority.

The reasons which prompted the general review of the system are found, for the most part, in the need to provide a public policy response to changes in the banking and financial industries.[197]

It has been observed, regarding this point, that the driving forces of the reform appear to have been public awareness and consumer protection. The attempt to bring the activity of the supervisory body back onto the rails of performing a public function (the above-mentioned public awareness) occurred through the introduction of the accountability – albeit mediated through the Ministry – of the supervisory authority towards parliament. This system is counter-balanced by a system of checks and measures aimed at guaranteeing the transparency of its work (consumer protection), with a system of participatory safeguards aimed at countering an excessive concentration of powers in the hands of the FSA.

Thus, within a system in which the structure of financial conglomerates is becoming increasingly important, (which, as described at length in the introductory chapter, constitutes both the *topos* and the effect of market dynamics) the Financial Services Authority was created, the single regulator with the function of guaranteeing regular and effective exchange of information with the authority assigned to the management of financial policy.[198]

The reorganisation of the market system through "compaction" of financial conglomerates brought about modification of the system, from self-regulation to uniform regulation by an external agent, which was given responsibility for supervision of financial markets.[199]

Enactment of the Financial Services and Markets Act on 18 June 2000 conferred legal legitimacy on the FSA. Established in 1997, at the urging of the Labour government, it

197 A. Cairncross, *La Banca d'Inghilterra: relazioni con il governo, la pubblica amministrazione e il Parlamento*, 40 e ss., in D. Masciandaro, S. Ristuccia, *L'autonomia della banche centrali*, Milano, 1988.

198 G. Consoli and I. De Santis, *Ruolo e funzioni delle Financial Services Authority, draft paper* pubblicato a cura del Ceradi, 2003, 7. See C. Briault, *Revising rationale for a single National Financial Service Regulator*, in *FSA Bulletin 2002/02*; E. Ferran, *Examining the United Kingdom's experience in adopting the single financial regulaltor model*, in *Brook. Journ. of International Law*, 2003, 257; *Financial Services Authority, A New Regulator for a New Millennium*, report available on www.fsa.gov.uk/pubs/policy/bnr_progress2.pdf, consulted in January 2008. L. Bartolini, *The Financial Services Authority: Structure, Mandate and Policy Issues, in IMF, Staff Country Report*, n. 99/44, Washington, 1999, 25.

199 P. Wood, *Financial conglomerates and conflicts of interests*, in *Conflicts of interest in the changing financial world*, London, 1987, 59, who lists the characteristics of financial conglomerates: "a banker financing the issuer of securities and owing the issuer duties of confidence and care; a dealer in securities for its own account; an investment adviser, owing duties to its client; a market maker dealing on its account; a manager of unit trusts and pension funds, owing duties to a specific client; a trustee of will trusts, owing duties to the beneficiaries of the estate; a corporate financial adviser, owing duties to the company; a trustee of debt or convertible issues, owing duties to the bond holders; an agent bank, owing duties to a syndicate of banks".

began operations in 1998, after the Bank of England Act 1998 assigned it responsibility for supervision of the stability of individual credit institutions.[200]

The first indication of the FSA's independence from political power may be found in the Act. Attachment 1, section 13 reads: "In relation to any of its functions a) the Authority is not to be regarded as acting on behalf of the Crown; b) its members, officers and staff are not to be regarded as Crown servants".[201]

Attachment 1, section 13 substantially provides for the FSA's nature as a limited liability company, thus excluding the possibility that any forms of liability could arise similar to those provided for in public administrations.

The model of limited liability company (LLC) seems to have developed from the North American system: it is almost completely without structure, because the shareholders are free to shape the internal organisation as they wish. The shareholders can limit their personal liability; the internal organisational structures and the methods of administration are those of a corporate model similar to the Italian *società di persone*.[202]

2. *The Authority's Structure*

The Financial Services Authority is a limited liability company, subject to the control of the Ministry of Finance (from here on referred to as the Treasury), although this control is formal. This is one of the aspects of the authority which is most noteworthy, because it denotes the hybrid character of the organisation. It must comply with the same rules followed by those subject to its supervision and, at the same time, it is charged with administering a public service, an aspect which places it in relationships with public authorities.

200 M. Mc Elwee – A. Tyrie, *Leviathan at Large. The new regulator for the financial markets, Centre for the policies study*, London, 2000, 2. *Public awareness and consumer protection are ruled by Articles* 4 and 5 of *Financial Services and Markets Act* (FSMA): "4. Public awareness (1) The public awareness objective is: promoting public understanding of the financial system. (2) It includes, in particular – (a) promoting awareness of the benefits and risks associated with different kinds of investment or other financial dealing; and (b) the provision of appropriate information and advice. (3) "The financial system" has the same meaning as in section 3. 5 The protection of consumers (1) The protection of consumers objective is: securing the appropriate degree of protection for consumers. (2) In considering what degree of protection may be appropriate, the Authority must have regard to – (a) the differing degrees of risk involved in different kinds of investment or other transaction; (b) the differing degrees of experience and expertise that different consumers may have in relation to different kinds of regulated activity; (c) the needs that consumers may have for advice and accurate information; and (d) the general principle that consumers should take responsibility for their decisions. (3) "Consumers" means persons – (a) who are consumers for the purposes of section 138; or (b) who, in relation to regulated activities carried on otherwise than by authorised persons, would be consumers for those purposes if the activities were carried on by authorised persons.

201 MC Elwee–Tyrie, *Leviathan at large. The new regulator of the financial markets*, London, 2000.

202 G. Riolfo, *Il sistema monistico di amministrazione e controllo delle società di capitali: il modello britannico e il modello nord-americano*, p. 284, in E. Pederzini, *Percorsi di diritto societario europeo*, Torino, 2007; G. Corradini, *Formulario commentato di contrattualistica commerciale Inghilterra-Italia*, Milano, 2000, 24–25.

As a company, it is a legal entity and is incorporated, similarly to a commercial company, where the directors act as agents of the shareholders and company relations are based on mutual trust.

Its structure does not present, in itself, any revolutionary aspects in comparison with previous supervisory models operating in the UK: at the top there is an Executive Chairman and it is managed by three Managing Directors. One of these is the head of the supervisory sector (in turn divided into banking, insurance, property companies and organisational sectors) and the other two manage respectively the structure which grants authorisations and issues sanctions, and the structure which is responsible for internal organisation.

As previously stated, the FSA is a limited liability company, where the Treasury has formal liability. In the relationship between the FSA and the public authorities there is also a link – again formal – with Parliament, to which a report on activities carried out is sent every year.

Thus the UK authority has ample room to manoeuvre, with strong limitation of its liability.

In order to gain a clear idea of the wide spectrum of powers granted to the FSA, it is useful to examine the contents of the opening sections of the Financial Services Market Act: authorisation, regulatory, consultative and sanctionative powers.[203]

This wide range of powers is counterbalanced by provision of a control mechanism, according to which the FSA may be subject to independent review. However it transpires from the provision, as we will see, that the aim of the law is not to hamper in reality the Authority's power to act.

The control referred to above may take different forms: supervision by the General Director of the Fair Trading and Competition Commission[204]; supervision by a

[203] See Article 2 of FSMA: "2. (2) The regulatory objectives are – (a) market confidence; (b) public awareness; (c) the protection of consumers; and (d) the reduction of financial crime. (3) In discharging its general functions the Authority must have regard to – (a) the need to use its resources in the most efficient and economic way; (b) the responsibilities of those who manage the affairs of authorized persons; (c) the principle that a burden or restriction which is imposed on a person, or on the carrying on of an activity, should be proportionate to the benefits, considered in general terms, which are expected to result from the imposition of that burden or restriction; (d) the desirability of facilitating innovation in connection with regulated activities; (e) the international character of financial services and markets and the desirability of maintaining the competitive position of the United Kingdom; (f) the need to minimize the adverse effects on competition that may arise from anything done in the discharge of those functions; (g) the desirability of facilitating competition between those who are subject to any form of regulation by the Authority. (4) The Authority's general functions are – (a) its function of making rules under this Act (considered as a whole); (b) its function of preparing and issuing codes under this Act (considered as a whole); (c) its functions in relation to the giving of general guidance (considered as a whole); and (d) its function of determining the general policy and principles by reference to which it performs particular functions".

[204] See Article 160 del FSMA: "160 Reports by Director General of Fair Trading (1) The Director must keep the regulating provisions and the Authority's practices under review. (2) If at any time the Director considers that – (a) a regulating provision or practice has a significantly adverse effect on competition, or (b) two or more regulating provisions or practices taken together, or a particular combination of regulating provisions and practices, have such an effect, he must make a report to that effect. (3) If at any time the Director considers that – (a) a regulating provision or practice does not have a significantly

completely independent Tribunal; or the faculty granted to the authority itself to review its own decisions and monitor itself.

The Court of Appeal, in a case submitted to it, specified that the powers of the Tribunal are exercised completely independently from the authority: "Its function is to hear and determine references from decisions of the authority. The Tribunal conducts a *de novo* review of the matters referred to it. It may consider evidence whether or not it was available to the authority at the material time. It may decide points of law, including disputes about the limits of its jurisdiction and the lawfulness of the decisions and actions of the authority".[205]

Finally, the Authority itself, during self-monitoring, may review its own decisions whenever its activity is subject to appraisal promoted by or on the initiative of the Treasury[206], which nominates an independent figure, or on the initiative of anyone who demonstrates an interest in such appraisal.

adverse effect on competition, or (b) two or more regulating provisions or practices taken together, or a particular combination of regulating provisions and practices, do not have any such effect, he may make a report to that effect. (4) A report under subsection (2) must include details of the adverse effect on competition. (5) If the Director makes a report under subsection (2) he must – (a) send a copy of it to the Treasury, the Competition Commission and the Authority; and (b) publish it in the way appearing to him to be best calculated to bring it to the attention of the public. (6) If the Director makes a report under subsection (3) – (a) he must send a copy of it to the Treasury, the Competition Commission and the Authority; and (b) he may publish it. (7) Before publishing a report under this section the Director must, so far as practicable, exclude any matter which relates to the private affairs of a particular individual the publication of which, in the opinion of the Director, would or might seriously and prejudicially affect his interests. (8) Before publishing such a report the Director must, so far as practicable, exclude any matter which relates to the affairs of a particular body the publication of which, in the opinion of the Director, would or might seriously and prejudicially affect its interests. (9) Subsections (7) and (8) do not apply in relation to copies of a report which the Director is required to send under subsection (5)(a) or (6)(a). (10) For the purposes of the law of defamation, absolute privilege attaches to any report of the Director under this section.

205 See *Regina (Davies and others) v. Financial Services Authority*, [2004] 1 *WLR* e [2003] *EWCA* (Civ) 1128. Article 132 del FSMA states as follows "The Financial Services and Markets Tribunal": 1) For the purposes of this Act, there is to be a tribunal known as the Financial Services and Markets Tribunal (but referred to in this Act as "the Tribunal"). (2) The Tribunal is to have the functions conferred on it by or under this Act. (3) The Lord Chancellor may by rules make such provision as appears to him to be necessary or expedient in respect of the conduct of proceedings before the Tribunal. (4) Schedule 13 is to have effect as respects the Tribunal and its proceedings [...]".

206 See Article 12 FSMA: "Reviews" (1) The Treasury may appoint an independent person to conduct a review of the economy, efficiency and effectiveness with which the Authority has used its resources in discharging its functions. (2) A review may be limited by the Treasury to such functions of the Authority (however described) as the Treasury may specify in appointing the person to conduct it. (3) A review is not to be concerned with the merits of the Authority's general policy or principles in pursuing regulatory objectives or in exercising functions under Part VI. (4) On completion of a review, the person conducting it must make a written report to the Treasury – (a) setting out the result of the review; and (b) making such recommendations (if any) as he considers appropriate. (5) A copy of the report must be – (a) laid before each House of Parliament; and (b) published in such manner as the Treasury consider appropriate. (6) Any expenses reasonably incurred in the conduct of a review are to be met by the Treasury out of money provided by Parliament. (7) "Independent" means appearing to the Treasury to be independent of the Authority. 13 Right to obtain documents and information (1) A person conducting a review under section 12 – (a) has a right of access at any reasonable time to all such documents as he may

The disposition according to which this control procedure must not enter into the merit of the choices made by the Authority reveals how ineffective this function really is, as it is reduced to the mere compiling of a report, subsequently transmitted to the Treasury.

Finally, the Treasury may order the establishment of independent committees of inquiry, that may perform a parallel activity to that of the Authority, should "serious failures of the system of regulation" occur.[207]

Analysis of the most recent financial scandals, to be discussed in greater depth in the section on liability, indicate that these measures have not produced the desired effects.

The safety net did not fall into place. Such an outcome is not surprising, considering the vague and unspecific nature of the dispositions mentioned above: the references to principles of efficiency and inexpensiveness, that should have become important criteria in assessment of the authority's operations, have certainly not helped to define the powers of control of the bodies charged with this assessment.

Evaluation of the strength of the British supervisory system is thus not very reassuring: if, in fact, the system was conceived and established in consequence of a clear, strong stimulus towards the creation of a model based on the efficiency and effectiveness of solutions in prudential supervision, this stimulus was not in itself sufficient to face the waves of crises which have washed across the British financial market.[208] Analysts were

reasonably require for purposes of the review; and (b) may require any person holding or accountable for any such document to provide such information and explanation as are reasonably necessary for that purpose. (2) Subsection (1) applies only to documents in the custody or under the control of the Authority. (3) An obligation imposed on a person as a result of the exercise of powers conferred by subsection (1) is enforceable by injunction or, in Scotland, by an order for specific performance under section 45 of the [1988 c. 36.] Court of Session Act 1988".

207 See Article 14 and 15 FSMA: "14. Cases in which the Treasury may arrange independent inquiries (1) This section applies in two cases. (2) The first is where it appears to the Treasury that – (a) events have occurred in relation to – (i) a collective investment scheme, or (ii) a person who is, or was at the time of the events, carrying on a regulated activity (whether or not as an authorised person), which posed or could have posed a grave risk to the financial system or caused or risked causing significant damage to the interests of consumers; and (b) those events might not have occurred, or the risk or damage might have been reduced, but for a serious failure in – (i) the system established by this Act for the regulation of such schemes or of such persons and their activities; or (ii) the operation of that system. (3) The second is where it appears to the Treasury that – (a) events have occurred in relation to listed securities or an issuer of listed securities which caused or could have caused significant damage to holders of liequilisted securities; and (b) those events might not have occurred but for a serious failure in the regulatory system established by Part VI or in its operation. (4) If the Treasury consider that it is in the public interest that there should be an independent inquiry into the events and the circumstances surrounding them, they may arrange for an inquiry to be held under section 15. (5) "Consumers" means persons – (a) who are consumers for the purposes of section 138; or (b) who, in relation to regulated activities carried on otherwise than by authorised persons, would be consumers for those purposes if the activities were carried on by authorised persons.

208 E. Ferran, *Examining the United Kingdom's experience in adopting the single financial regulator model cit.*, 290: "effectiveness is measured by whether a regulatory system achieves its objectives. Effectiveness overlaps with suitability – a single regulator may be more effective than alternative regulatory models because its structure is better suited to the increasingly integrated nature of financial markets. [...] Effectiveness also overlaps with efficiency because inefficient regulation is likely to produce results that are inimical to a properly effective system of regulation".

prepared to swear that the FSA was indestructible when faced with the shock wave of financial crises: some spoke of the "FSA's recipe for success, difficult to copy", in the "difficult balance between principles and rules". Reality has surpassed imagination and the house of cards rapidly collapsed, only to be subsequently rebuilt (unfortunately, exposed to the same winds and built with the same cards).

In addition there are the possible consequences that excessive concentration of powers in the hands of a single body may have; this concentration may be detrimental both to its impartiality and its independence.

It should also be remembered that, although the FSA has gained the favour of external observers, on the internal front, however, concerns began to emerge soon after the enactment of the FSMA. These were prevalently related to the weak definition of liability delegated to a regulator which, operating without any effective controls, is endowed with dangerously Draconian powers.[209]

In other words, the decision to give this authority rather unclearly-defined control of financial operations of a risky and unprincipled nature was a source of concern.[210]

As previously stated, the authority was provided with broad powers in taking disciplinary procedures and in inflicting sanctions, to the point that it could be considered simultaneously as "prosecutor, judge and jury".[211]

In this case, as for the Italian and German systems, Community law and the Basel standards acted as a balancing force.

3. *MiFID and Basel II: the FSA reaction*

A counterweight to the excessive concentration of powers in the hands of the FSA seems to derive from the Community network, and particularly from compliance with the duty of cooperation between authorities that the FSA is also bound to. The authority's obligation emerges from the considerations made on the Green Paper on Financial Services Policy for the years 2005–2010.

The commentary of the Financial Services Authority in this document is organised around five main points. The first consideration concerns the requirement to implement *ex post* Community directives and oversee their effective application. This means that the directives must not only be correctly transposed, but also adequately applied by the

209 E. Ferran, *Examining the United Kingdom's Experience cit.*, 296: "about accountability in relation to single regulators because of the all-embracing nature of their role and their concentrated and potentially draconian powers" G. Parkinson, *FSA Bows Criticisms of Being Judge and Jury in Enforcement Regime, Money Marketing*, July 8, 1999, 2; D. Atkinsons, *"Judge, Jury and Executioner", Clims Defeat City Super Regulator, Guardian*, July 6, 1999, 22.

210 M. Ojo, *The Financial Services Authority: A Model of Improved Accountability?*, in http://mpra.ub.uni-muenchen.de/228/1/MPRA_paper_ 228.pdf, consulted in January 2008: "Can a single regulator be made properly accountable to an industry while avoiding regulatory capture? Can it be made properly accountable to consumers without creating false perceptions and possible moral hazard concerns about the extent to which the regulatory system will protect them from financial risks?". And furthermore "if the single regulator is independent of government [...], by what mechanisms can it be held politically accountable in respect of its public interest functions?".

211 M. Boleat, *The Abi View*, in *Financial World*, 1999, 24.

competent national agencies. Point 5 of the annual report reads: "First, we welcome the general approach contained in the Green Paper, in particular the reaffirmation that the key task now is to complete the existing legislative initiatives, and to embark on new ones only where there is robust evidence that they would address an existing market failure in a cost effective manner. We also welcome the commitment to ensuring that Community obligations are not merely transposed correctly but also properly applied by national competent authorities. We also welcome the proposal that existing directives should be subject to continuous *ex-post* evaluation".

Secondly, the FSA, in examining global supervisory models, regards the North American system as one not to be replicated. It aims to reinforce a system of rules whose main objective is to prevent the failure of corporate governance, and it may be excessively restrictive: "Recent history suggests that the traditionally highly prescriptive US approach has been ineffective in preventing corporate governance failures in the real world, and it is not clear that further prescriptive measures would be effective in preventing future abuse, particularly if applied in a non-risk based way. We therefore do not consider that the US model is one which the EU should replicate".

Thirdly, according to UK analysts, it is necessary to continue to encourage the initiatives of the Lamfalussy Committee, for example by creating a single regulator of the global system, through the commitment of stakeholders and a strategic agreement on the costs and benefits of common objectives: "Third, we welcome the continued endorsement of the Lamfalussy structures [...] in ensuring that significant internationally active financial services institutions and market structures are subject to an effectively co-ordinated set of managed regulatory relationships. This should lead to a significant reduction in regulatory duplication [...] This would certainly require the commitment of huge resources by all stakeholders and the consolidation proposal would be of limited value without the simultaneous alignment of contract and insolvency law. A proper cost-benefit assessment of such a large programme of work would be essential before embarking on it".

Fourthly, the FSA suggests providing incentives, primarily in those sectors in which supervision seems to be crucial, that is where there are real risks of instability and where it is necessary to guarantee a high level of consumer protection: "Fourth, there are suggestions in the Green Paper that the extent to which the objective of creating a single market has been met, should be evidenced by the extent to which financial services are provided cross-border. We suggest below that a better test should be whether there are significant barriers to a free flow of goods and services. But there is a further point which we consider is relevant in assessing how to prioritise areas where action may be indicated, namely the effect of any measure on the risks to financial stability and consumer protection" (point 2.7).

Finally, in alignment with the idea which foundered with the European Constitution but was proposed again more recently (in particular with the Treaty of Lisbon) of promoting the role of national parliaments, encouragement is made to wield the instrument of agreements reached through the committees with the legislation of the individual States: "Fifth, in the event that the European Constitution is not ratified, we consider it essential that priority be given, either in the context of comitology generally or the Lamfalussy arrangements specifically, to settling the question of the Parliament's role in relation to delegated 'level 2' legislation, in order that the relevant provisions in the various Lamfalussy directives can be renewed" (point 2.10).

4. *Interlude*

In an interlude between acts of a more serious nature, here is some light entertainment to raise the morale of the audience.

October 1907. "The Knickerbocker Trust Company was a renowned institution in America's Gilded Age, the golden era at the beginning of the 20th century. In those roaring years of extremely rapid economic growth, many New York middle class families entrusted their savings to this prestigious finance company which had its headquarters on the corner between the Fifth Avenue and 34th Street, in front of the Waldorf Astoria Hotel. How could one possibly not trust this institute? Heading the Knickerbocker company was Charles Tracy Barney, married to a Whitney (of the museum family), member of thirty three boards of directors of industrial giants, private investor in the construction of the Manhattan Subway: a Great Gatsby of the American capitalist establishment. With the economy growing at a yearly rate of seven percent, between 1896 and 1906 the US GDP had doubled, and returns on investments were generous. The 'American century' was starting under extremely favourable auspices. However, the unstoppable rise of the new world power was not to occur without any setbacks. A hundred years ago, the great panic of 1907 was the first 'global' economic crisis of the 20th century. In the month of October alone, Wall Street's stock index lost thirty seven percent of its value, and all around the country hoards of investors stormed bank counters amid scenes of violence and desperation. The credit system remained paralysed for weeks. [...] On October 24, with Wall Street closed for lack of trade and a wave of panic crossing the oceans to engulf both Europe and Asia, all the brokers of the New York stock exchange flocked like pilgrims to the headquarters of J.P Morgan to ask the great banker for advice. 'Mr. Morgan, we will have to close the stock exchange', the senior broker whispered, meaning close it indefinitely. Morgan abruptly answered: 'You will close it at the correct hour. Three in the afternoon, not a minute earlier'. He then began to fill out cheques, personally, for each and every broker, to give them enough liquidity and to ensure that money would start flowing again in the Stock Exchange. At this point the tycoon John Rockefeller made his contribution. Morgan had directed the system's bailout operations, and then Rockefeller supplied him with fifty million dollars of his personal fortune within a matter of hours. Morgan wired instructions to partners in the City of London, explaining that the global financial system was in danger. On his orders the Lusitania set sail from England with a historically unique cargo: the largest quantity of gold ingots ever transported across the Atlantic. The mass panic died down. America was safe".[212]

212 F. Rampini, *Crack 1907, la tempesta perfetta*, in *La Domenica di Repubblica*, 14 October 2007, pp. 36–37: "La Knickerbocker Trust Company era un'istituzione celebre nell'America della Gilded Age, l'età dell'oro del primo Novecento. In quegli anni ruggenti, dallo sviluppo economico accelerato, molte famiglie del ceto medio newyorchese avevano affidato i propri risparmi alla prestigiosa società

October 2007- March 2008: "London – a *mea culpa* with no extenuating circumstances: the Financial Services Authority, the watchdog for the British financial markets, admitted today that it had failed in its task and had not monitored the situation at Northern Rock. In a long-awaited report published today, Wednesday March 26, the FSA, dressed in sackcloth and ashes, lists a series of mistakes which led to the liquidity crisis of the mortgage lending bank which, last summer, became the most prominent British victim of the financial catastrophe that originated with the subprime mortgage scandal in the United States. The source of all the errors was an 'unacceptable lack of supervision and controls', the FSA admitted. The number of officials assigned to Northern Rock was too small, controls were not sufficiently rigorous or frequent, requests for information and details from bank management were sporadic. [...] Northern Rock rapidly grew in a few years by using the aggressive strategy of securing market share by offering mortgages at advantageous conditions and loans of as much as 125% of the property's value. It accumulated more than 110 billion pounds in assets, making it the eighth bank and the fifth mortgage provider in Britain. Its business model, based on the strategy of counting on capital markets to raise finance rather than on clients' deposits, was well known to the FSA. Nevertheless, even though it had all the distinctive features of a company which needed to be under special supervision by the FSA, the report shows how Northern Rock was, instead, subject to less supervision and fewer controls than other more stable banks. At the root of the problem there also seems to have been a lack of communication and a

finanziaria con sede all'angolo fra la Quinta Avenue e la 34esima strada, dirimpetto all'Hotel Waldorf Astoria. E come non fidarsi? Al vertice della Knickerbocker c'era Charles Tracy Barney, sposato con una Whitney (quelli del museo), membro di trentatré consigli d'amministrazione di colossi industriali, finanziatore in proprio della costruzione del metrò di Manhattan: un Grande Gatsby dell'establishment capitalistico americano. Con un'economia che cresceva a ritmi del sette per cento annuo, tra il 1896 e il 1906 il Pil degli Stati Uniti si era raddoppiato, i rendimenti offerti ai risparmiatori erano generosi. Si apriva sotto i migliori auspici il 'secolo americano'. Ma l'irresistibile ascesa della nuova potenza mondiale non sarebbe avvenuta senza scossoni. Cent'anni fa il grande panico del 1907 fu la prima crisi 'globale' del Novecento. Nel solo mese di ottobre l'indice azionario di Wall Street perse il trentasette per cento del suo valore, in tutta l'America folle di risparmiatori diedero l'assalto agli sportelli delle banche fra scene di violenza e di disperazione, il sistema del credito rimase paralizzato per settimane. [...] Il 24 ottobre, mentre Wall Street è ferma per mancanza di contrattazioni e l'onda di paura traversa gli oceani coinvolgendo Europa ed Asia, tutti i broker della Borsa newyorchese affluiscono in pellegrinaggio al quartier generale della J.P. Morgan per chiedere consiglio al grande banchiere. 'Mr. Morgan – gli sussurra il decano dei broker – dovremo chiudere lo Stock Exchange'. Intende dire: a tempo indeterminato. Morgan risponde secco: 'Lo chiuderete come tutti i giorni all'orario canonico. Le tre del pomeriggio, non un secondo prima'. E si mette a riempire assegni, lui di persona, per ciascuno dei broker. Perché abbiano liquidità sufficiente e il denaro torni a scorrere nello Stock Exchange. A quel punto si fa vivo il magnate John Rockefeller con un messaggio lapidario. Se è Morgan a guidare le operazioni di salvataggio del sistema, Rockefeller gli farà avere cinquanta milioni di dollari dal suo patrimonio personale in poche ore. Morgan telegrafa istruzioni anche ai partner nella City di Londra, spiega che è la finanza mondiale in pericolo. Ai suoi ordini salpa dall'Inghilterra il bastimento Lusitania con un carico unico nella storia: il più grande quantitativo di lingotti d'oro mai trasportato attraverso l'Atlantico. La psicosi di massa si dilegua. L'America è salva".

radical difference of opinions between the Bank of England and the FSA: the Authority delayed intervening as it should have done last summer".[213]

Two episodes, one hundred years apart. Two financial crises recurred with rather disturbing similarities, also in their solutions: the lifeline, the lender in the last resort, whose role will be further examined later on in the conclusion to this dissertation. A rich, trusted and unscrupulous financier in the first case; the United Kingdom in the first and second case. In the latter crisis the FSA played an entirely secondary role. It asked to be pardoned for not having supervised, for its slowness (although really the word that should be used is failure) to intervene. Now the question arises as to what kind of liability may exist in such a case, and if independent authorities in the UK system are liable for the damage they cause to private citizens.

In order to answer this question it will be necessary to analyse the UK system of liability, with a brief look at the American model (founded on the ashes of the 1907 financial crisis) as well, on which it was based.

Section 2. Liability (With a view towards the US)

1. *Overview of the US model*

Analysis of the system of liability of US supervisory authorities is necessary in order to understand how the British system works. The US Independent Regulatory Commissions constitute, in fact, the basis for a "functional model" of authorities that has influenced the British model and which has been at the centre of much debate as regards its applicability in other European systems.[214]

In the United States, the need for a system of controls over the operations of banking institutions first emerged in a sensational manner after the severe financial crisis of 1907; Congress decided to establish a system aimed at absorbing shocks caused by the poor management of banking and credit activity, under the aegis of the Federal Reserve Bank.[215]

The Federal Reserve System, within which the activity of the Federal Reserve Bank is included, constitutes a typical example of an Independent Agency, with functions of supervision and control over the banking system.

213 E. Franceschini, *Northern Rock? Senza fondo...*, in *Repubblica* 3 December 2007; N. Segli Innocenti, *La Consob inglese: su Northern Rock abbiamo fallito*, in www.ilsole24ore.com/homepage.shtm. See A. Greco, *Retata Fbi a Wall Street per i mutui subprime*, in *Repubblica*, 20 June 2008, p. 26.

214 F. Merusi, M. Passaro, *Autorità indipendenti*, in *Enc. dir.*, Aggiornamento, VI, Milano, 2003, 190; E. Bellini, Class actions *e mercato finanziario: l'esperienza nordamericana*, in *Danno e resp.*, 2005, 817.

215 Seban, *Le juge administratif cit.*; on US regulation: D. Mulligan, *Know your customer regulations and the international banking system: towards a general self-regulatory regime*, in *Fordham International Journal Law*, 1999, 2324; S.G. Brayer, R.B. Stewart, C.R. Sunstein, M.L. Spitzer, *Administrative Law and Regulatory Policy*, New York, 2002, 19; C.P. Guarini, in *Contributo allo studio della regolazione "indipendente"*, Bari, 2005, pp. 163–174.

In the United States, the administrative system corresponding to our notion of public administration is composed of a series of bodies that are generally referred to as agencies. Thus, the term "agency" becomes synonymous with administration, in accordance with the system provided for by the Constitution.

The activity of agencies is, in fact, considered as a manifestation both of the President's executive power and of the legislative power held by Congress; in this manner, the authorities take on a role as agents of the legislative power delegated to them.

Studies have highlighted the obvious difficulties of such a subdivision of powers, observing how the "two-faceted" nature of these agencies, which pursue simultaneously two distinct political and institutional objectives, determines a series of problematic consequences within the US system.[216]

This situation is further complicated by the fact that identification of the agencies' duties is accomplished by generically defining the results to be achieved; this policy leaves them ample discretion on the choice of possible policy options.

Thus supervision over the correctness of the agencies' operations meets two significant limits. On the one hand, there is the obvious difficulty, from a practical point of view, of defining the agencies losses; on the other hand, there are the heavy restrictions at a legislative level on recognising the liability of the supervisory and controlling authorities, if they acted "in the exercise of a discretional power".

The Federal Government's liability, in the event of unlawful conduct by the agencies, is regulated by the Federal Tort Claims Act[217], in particular by Sections 2671 to 2680 of Article 171.

Section 2671 gives a definition of Federal Agency, including executive and legislative departments, military departments, the independent institutions of the United States and the corporations that act instrumentally or by means of an agency relationship with the United States. But the notion does not extend to any contracting party[218]: "[...] [T]he term 'federal agency' includes the executive departments, the judicial and legislative branches, the military departments, independent establishments of the United States, and corporations primarily acting as instrumentalities or agencies of the United States, but does not include any contractor with the United States".[219]

Section 2675 specifies the cases in which a liability lawsuit against federal authorities may be initiated, introducing, as a condition for the admissibility of the legal action, the formula of prior fulfilment of "internal recourse", but with a rather predictable further condition. Silent denial is possible in cases where the Federal Agency cited has not decided by six months after the claim was made: "(a) An action shall not be instituted upon a claim against the United States for money damages for injury or loss of property

216 L. Barra Caracciolo, *Funzione amministrativa e amministrazione neutrale nell'ordinamento U.S.A. Profili comparativi con l'esperienza italiana*, Torino, 1997, 26.

217 USCA §§2671–2680.

218 R.D. Hejl, Plaintiff-Appellant, v. United States of America et al., Defendants-Appellees. No. 71–2111 United States Court of Appeals, Fifth Circuit, available in Federal Reporter, vol. 449, II ed., September-November 1971 and furthermore on http://bulk.resource.org/courts.gov/c/F2/449/449.F2d.124.71-2111_1.html, consulted in April 2008.

219 §2671 USCA.

or personal injury caused by the negligent or wrongful act or omission of any employee of the Government while acting within the scope of his office or employment, unless the claimant shall have first presented the claim to the appropriate Federal agency and his claim shall have been finally denied by the agency in writing and sent by certified or registered mail. The failure of an agency to make final deposition of a claim within six months after it is filed shall, at the option of the claimant any time thereafter, be deemed a final denial of the claim for purposes of this section". The so-called internal recourse "in opposition" constitutes a element which may be evaluated by the judge on penalty of the admissibility of the claim, assessable by the judge and, therefore, it represents a not insignificant limit to the possibility of initiating a legal claim.

Thus we can see that the aggrieved party may encounter some difficulty in proving not only that there is a causal relationship between damage suffered and the agency's unlawful conduct in the person of the officer responsible, but also that this conduct does not come under the public administration's discretionary power. Section 2680, among the grounds for excluding liability, expressly provides for the possibility of an agency fulfilling a "discretionary function". The range of liability, in fact, does not include the cases in which a public function is performed by a federal officer or by a government employee. Section 2680 "shall not apply to...any claim ... based upon the exercise or performance of discretionary function or duty on the part of a federal agency or an employee of the Government, whether or not the discretion involved be abused".[220]

Furthermore, the Supreme Court, in a renowned adjudication in 1991[221], did not hesitate to declare the indisputability of rules put in place by the Federal Reserve, on the grounds of the alleged discretionary nature of the power it exercises.

The case in question regarded a liability claim made against the United States of America by the General Director of the Independent American Savings Association (IASA), Thomas A. Gaubert, majority shareholder of the company. He made a claim for damage suffered as a result of failure to oversee IASA. The damage was caused by two

220 On *vicarius liability*, see B. Markesinis – S. Deakin, *Tort Law*, Oxford University Press, 1999, 532. On the interpretation of that clause see *Fisher Bros. Sales Inch. et al. vs United States of America*, where its was stated that "the decisions were policy decisions protected by discretionary function exception to the FTCA. [...] The FDA acted to protect the public from the risk of exposure to poisonous fruit which it learned colud be coming from Chile. It had the discretion to test the fruit and determine whether the fruit was adultered. It also had the discretion to refuse entry into the United States. The actions taken were not violative of any regulatory or statutory provisions". Conf. United States vs. S.A. Empresa De Viacao Aerea Rio Grandense (Varig Airlines), 467 U.S. 797, 808 (1984), which stated that "whathever else the discretionary power function exception may include, it plainly was intended to encompass the discretionary acts of the Government acting in its role as a regulator of the conduct of private individuals. Time and again the legislative history refers to the acts of regulatory agencies as examples of those covered by the exception". See again *Eugene Dupree, Appellant, v. United States*. No. 12617. United States Court of Appeals Third Circuit, in Federal Reporter, II ed., March 1959, available at http://bulk.resource.org/courts.gov/c/F2/264/264.F2d.140.12617_1.html.

221 *United States vs. Gaubert*, 499 U.S., 315 (1991), available at http://laws. findlaw.com/us/499/315.html. See also: *Ellen R. Hibble vs. United States* 97–2077 (1997), *Faber vs. United States* 56 F. 3d 1122, 1123, 1126–1128 (1995); *Andrulonis vs. United States*, 952 F. 2d 652, 655 (1991). More recently, *KISKA Construction Corporation U.S.A. Et al. vs. Washington Metropolitan Area Transit Authority* 01–7156 (2003).

banks, which, after having unsuccessfully tried to oust him from his position, had taken over management of the company. Mr. Gaubert was forced to yield to pressure to resign from his position as company chairman, pressure which the two mortgage lending banks, the Federal Home Loan Bank Board (FHLBB) and the Federal Home Loan Bank Bord-Dallas (FHLBB-D) had exerted on him in order to gain greater control in IASA. Mr. Gaubert, faced with the overbearing behaviour of the two banks, initiated a damages claim in the District Court against them for mismanagement of IASA's affairs. The defence that these two banks used to counter the accusations was based on the discretionary power of their actions, which were, according to them, part of their public policy function. At appeal, the Court of Appeal considered the actions of the new management to be "operational actions" and not "policy decisions".[222]

Section 1 of the Court's reasons states that the discretionary function exception applies to all cases in which an element of judgement or choice are based on considerations of public interest: "The discretionary function exception covers acts involving an element of judgement or choice if they are based on considerations of public policy".[223]

It is, therefore, on the basis of the nature of the conduct, and not on the qualifications of the acting party, that evaluation of possible application of the discretionary power exception is based: "It is the nature of the conduct rather than the status of the actor, that governs whether the exception applies".[224]

In addition, such exception applies to all cases in which the agent's action is based on grounds of a social, economic or political character. Therefore if an agent acts in conformity with the dispositions of a mandatory regulation, the government will not be held liable for the actions carried out. However, if the public official breaches this regulation, his action will not be immune from liability, because its binding nature, by definition, does not attribute any margin of choice to the official (the expression "there is no room for choice" confirms this). Thus the action will be seen as in conflict with public interest or public policy: "In addition to protecting policymaking or planning functions and the promulgation of regulations to carry out programs, the exception also protects Government agents' actions involving the necessary element of choice and grounded in the social, economic, or political goals of a statute and regulations. If an employee obeys the direction of a mandatory regulation, the Government will be protected because the action will be deemed in furtherance of the policies which led to the regulation's promulgation; and if an employee violates a mandatory regulation, there will be no shelter from liability, because there is no room for choice, and the action will be contrary to policy [...]. On the other hand, when established governmental policy, as expressed or implied by statute, regulation or agency guidelines, allows a Government agent to exercise discretion, there is a strong presumption that the agent's acts are grounded in policy when exercising that discretion".[225]

222 Indian Towing, Co., Inc., v. United States, 350 U.S. 61 (1955), on http://supreme.justia.com/us/350/61/case.html.

223 United States v. Gaubert, 499 U.S., 315 (1991), *cit.*, §1.

224 Idem.

225 United States v. Gaubert *cit.*, Held 1.

The exemption of the supervisory bodies from any sort of liability is thus consecrated by a syllogism in which the primary premise (indisputability of actions taken in exercising a discretionary power), secondary premise (discretional nature of powers exercised by the agencies) and conclusion (impossibility of subjecting the activity of agencies to jurisdictional control) follow each other in perfect logical order.[226]

The weak link in the chain lies hidden in the expression "discretionary function", which seems to correspond to technical discretion. If this is the case, it may become increasingly difficult to continue to claim the indisputability of agencies' actions.[227]

2. *The system of regulatory agencies in the UK*

Similarly to Germany and the United States Britain has always appeared to be fairly reluctant to allow the possibility of initiating liability claims against supervisory authorities. The rare cases submitted to the judgement of the courts and the repeated attempts of the British Parliament to neutralise a potential "liability risk" through the provision of "partial immunity liability" are indicators of an approach which is clearly biased towards protecting the work of the supervisory authorities.

One example of this may be seen in the Banking Act, enacted in 1987[228], and modifying Article 17 of the Constitution of the Bank of England. It explicitly excludes the banking institute and the members of the board of directives, be they officials or employees, from being responsible for damage suffered by third parties in relation to acts, facts or negligence performed when carrying out the functions provided for by the Banking law, aside from cases of misfeasance.[229]

As previously mentioned, British law also tends to reject the possibility that bodies supervising banks and credit institutions may be liable. A substantial tightening of the United Kingdom's approach occurred with the decision in Yuen-Kun-yeu vs. Attorney General of Hong Kong[230], in 1987, in which the Privy Council rejected as inadmissible the damages claim brought by a group of investors against Hong Kong's Authority for banking supervision for negligence in oversight of the operations of credit institutions. The Privy Council argued that liability "can only be conceived when a sufficient proximity existed between the supervisory authorities and the bank creditors, such as to legitimate a duty of care of the former towards the latter".[231]

226 W.J. Carney, *Jurisdictional Choice in Securities Regulation*, in *Virginia Journal of International Law*, 2001, 718.

227 M. Argentati, *Il sindacato giurisdzionale sulla autorità indipendenti nell'esperienza statunitense e italiana*, in F. Francario (cur. by), *Diritti, interessi ed amministrazioni indipendenti. Giornate di studio sulla giustizia amministrativa dedicate ad Eugenio Cannada-Bartoli*, Giuffré, 2003, 185.

228 Penn, *Banking Supervision. Regulation of the UK banking Sector under the Banking Act 1987*, London, Butterworths, 1989, 22. About *Bank of England see on* www.bankofengland.co.uk.

229 Seban, *Le juge administratif cit.*, 2.

230 *Yuen Kun Yu vs. Attorney General of Hong Kong* [1988] AC 175.

231 Conf. *Davis vs. Ratcliffe* [1990], I, WLR, 821. Both the judgments are quoted in Three Rivers DC vs. Bank of England (No 3), [2003] 2 AC, 103, as examples of *negligence cases where it has been stated that* "public regulators who had discretionary powers to stop deposit-taking institutions from carrying in business, but non day to day control or supervision of them, had no legal responsibility to depositors or

The intentionally vague character of the expression "sufficient proximity" does not seem very different from the vagueness of the notion of "public interest" stipulated as a condition to proceed by section 2680 of the FTCA: in the British system, as in the US system, there seems to be a lack of clarity that impedes recognition of full protection to parties damaged by the activity of independent administrative bodies.

In the attempt to limit an excessive increase in possible exemptions from liability, the Financial Services and Market Act was approved in 2000. This legislation unified all the bodies of financial supervision in the Financial Services Authority (FSA), and established that the system of immunity does not stop investors from being able to make claims, if the bad faith of the supervisory organ can be demonstrated.[232]

3. *The effects of legislation on case law*

The Queen's Bench Division and the Court of Appeal have both conformed to the provisions of the law, if only in a formal manner, by drawing on the notion of "misfeasance in public office"[233] and, in this way, assimilating the concept of bad faith with that of misfeasance.[234]

The House of Lords also had the opportunity to give an opinion on misfeasance in public office, providing interesting reconstructive insights.

The dispute originated from a claim initiated by approximately six thousand investors, as a result of the collapse of the BCCI (Bank of Credit and Commerce International), against the Bank of England, with the objective of gaining compensation for the damage caused by its failure of oversight, given its "principal responsibility for supervising banking activities in the United Kingdom".

The problems faced by the judges in this particular case are manifold; here we will look at two aspects of this complex question.

Firstly, the case is interesting as regards the definition of the concept of misfeasance in public office, given its extremely weak contours; secondly, there is the controversial

potential depositors for default of those institutions made possible as a result of their regulatory decisions, even though one of their functions was to protect depositors" (Audl LJ). Lord Auld (Three Rivers cit., p. 108) observes that "the primary question in both Privy Council Cases was whether there was a duty of care: the Yuen case, per Lord Keith, at p190C-D; David v Radcliffe, per Lord Goff, at pp. 825–826; 826–827. In both the Judicial Committee determined it according to common law criteria as to the presence or absence of a close and direct relationship between regulator and depositors and of a special relationship between the regulator and the deposit-taking institutions concerned, and by reference to public policy considerations governing the exercise by public body of a discretion". See R. Caranta, in *Governmental Liability after Francovich*, in [1993] *Camb.* L.J. 272; and in H.-W. Micklitz – S. Weatherill (eds.), *European Economic Law*, Ashgate, Dartmouth, 1997, 495: "the claim was rejected on the ground that even if harm to customers was a forseeable consequence of allowing unsound banks to continue in business, foreseeability alone was insufficient to establish a duty, no such duty being owed by the authority to individual customers, since its powers and duties were conferred in the interest of the public at large".

232 M. Tison, *Challenging the Prudential Supervisor cit.*, 13.

233 E.P. Ellinger, E. Lomnicka, *Modern Banking Law*, 2nd ed., Oxford, Clarendon Press, 1994, 32.

234 C. Proctor, *Financial regulators – Risks and liabilities*, in *Butterworths Journal of International Banking and Financial Law*, 2002, 19.

issue concerning the coordination of national legislation with Community directives, especially with Directive 77/780 EEC.

As regards the first point, Lord Hirst's speech is significant.[235] Referring to the conclusions already expressed in a previous case[236], he identifies a strong link between the tort of misfeasance and the notion of abuse ("the tort of misfeasance in public office is concerned with an abuse, or deliberately wrongful use, of the powers given to a public officer").

The subsequent step, according to the judge, consists in searching for the different nuances that the subjective element of tort may acquire. The concept of tort may, in fact, extend to the notion of intentional tort, but it may also take on the characteristics of what may be called "conscious negligence" ("an officer must also have known that his actions would probably injure the plaintiff"), or, ultimately, of gross negligence ("alternatively, it is sufficient for the plaintiff to show that the public officer was reckless or indifferent as to whether his acts or omissions would or might result in loss or damage to the plaintiff or to a person or persons in a class of which the plaintiff was a member").[237]

The distinction between lawful and unlawful activity is indicated by the degree of awareness underlying the conduct. According to Lord Hirst, "the concern is, and should only be, to ensure that a public officer who makes an honest attempt to exercise his powers but who, as a result of some mistake, acts unlawfully, is protected from liability". Liability may only subsist in the event that the "public officer [...] knowingly acts unlawfully".

The greatest difficulty emerging from analysis of case law is the changeable nature of the problems connected with liability. As Lord Hirst said: "the law on misfeasance in public office is not set in stone, and [...] it is susceptible of judicial development in the time-honoured tradition of the common law, particularly as the tort has a potential application in such a wide variety of circumstances affecting an extensive range of authorities. It follows that in our judgement we should not be unduly prescriptive in defining the ingredients of tort".[238]

The second point which deserves attention regards the applicability of Directive 77/780 to the area in question and, more generally, the impact of Community directives on the law of Member States.

In the cases described, the position held by the Lords rapidly moves towards the principle of the primacy of Community dispositions over national law which may even be in contrast with them.

235 *Three Rivers DC vs. Bank of England* (No 3) (CA) *cit.*, 26.

236 *Bourgoin SA vs. Ministry of Agriculture, Fisheries and Food* [1986] QB 716.

237 Lord Hirst explains how flexible the boundaries of the tort are: "liability will arise in any case where there has been an abuse, or a deliberately or recklessly wrongful use, of the powers given to a public officer. The boundaries of the tort are not tightly drawn and there is scope for future development". *Three Rivers cit.*, 27.

238 Lord Steyn (Three Rivers *cit.* (HL), 191): 1) *The defendant must be a public officer*; 2) *He must exercise the power as a public officer*; 3) *State of mind of the public officer.*

As is well-known, this feature of the dispositions contained in the Treaties was first recognised by the rulings in Van Gend en Loos and Costa vs. Enel.[239]

The second important aspect that deserves mention concerns the recognition by Community law of the so-called direct effect of directives on national systems, when they lay specific and unconditional obligations on the Member States.[240]

It is precisely within these two coordinates (primacy and direct effect) that the principle has developed, also arising from case law, of State liability for failure to implement directives and the consequent emergence of an obligation to compensate.

In particular, the argument (made for the first time with the verdict in the Francovich v. Repubblica Iitaliana case, and upheld subsequently by the rulings in the Lomas, Brasserie du Pêcheur, Factortame, and Dillenkofer cases) in which the Court, developing the principle first established in 1991, declared that the possibility of Member State liability is, in any case, subordinated to the existence of three conditions: the attribution by the Directive of a right held by the single individual in a clear and unconditional manner; serious and manifest breach of the directive; existence of a direct causal relationship between the breach committed by the State and the damage suffered.

The process of verification of the existence of these three requirements was also carried out by the Court of Appeal and by the House of Lords, in the case being discussed.[241]

The judgment, which had been almost unanimously favourable in the Appeal Court, was overruled by the final judges, on the grounds of lack of attribution of rights in favour of single investors.

239 ECJ, 5 February 1963, C-26/62, in *OJ.* 1963, 1, in *Giur. it.*, 1963, IV, 49, note Gori, *Una pietra miliare nell'affermazione del diritto europeo*; ECJ, 14 July 1964, C-6/64, in *OJ.*, 1964, 1127, in *Giur. it.*, 1964, I, 1073.

240 ECJ, 17 October, 1989, joint cases C-231/87 e C-129/88, Carpaneto Piacentino, in *OJ*, 1989 I, 3233; Id., 23 February 1994, C-236/92, *ivi*, 1994, I, 483; Id., 20 April 1999, C-241/97, *ivi*, 1999, I, 1896.

241 See Lord Hope Craighed's opinion [2003] 2 AC, 218, 1996 (Clarke J. [1996] 3All ER 558, 616: "the true position ... is that the Directive was not intended to require the imposition of a duty to supervise upon the supervisory authority". Conf. *Regina v. International Stock Exchange of the United Kingdom and the Republic of Ireland Ltd.*, [1993] (QB), 534.

SECOND READING

"As in Paris after Thermidor, and in London after the Armistice of 1918, Vienna danced throughout the autumn and all through the winter, while the Corsican was safe on the island of Elba and the authorities were shaping a new Europe".

These are the words of H.A.L. Fischer on the Congress of Vienna. After the great fear of the revolution[242], the European aristocracy abandoned itself to an orgy of profligacy in which dynastic interests and the exigencies of the national interests coexisted with the highest expressions of art.

Vienna, 1815. Basel, 2007. After great fear and trembling, after collapse and instability, and national interest sacrificed at the altar of other – or only better disguised – interests, history repeats itself.

The elite continue to meet in order to define the boundaries of the superpowers.

Rereading and re-assessing a text is both a difficult but necessary task, in order to render justice to years of work and understand the value of this effort. The comparison between the systems of the German and British supervisory authorities enables identification of numerous common features. These include, put extremely simply, the need to standardise systems of supervision, to provide safety nets to protect us in times of financial downturns.

These models, however, are also part of a wider sphere, today generally defined as "global". The global market is nothing more than a reproduction on a larger scale of the dynamics of local or regional markets, whose systems and structures it develops and combines. On a global level there seems to be no authority which is able to stand above all the others, or at least the idea of sovereignty traditionally associated with the triad state-people-territory is missing. This, however is just the upper misleading layer of the global community. More careful observation of what lies below reveals that this is not the case. The States, or the political choices which guide them, are not slow to appear on the canvas of the global system.

In the end the policies of strong States are even more evident than their geographical boundaries. Indeed they may give to this sovereignty even greater strength, because they enable these states to go beyond geographical limits and barriers. It is the superpowers,

[242] S. Guarracino, P. Ortoleva, M. Revelli, *Storia dell'età moderna*, Milano, 1993, 656.

meeting in grand financial cities, who decide the destinies that other powers, or other derivations of powers, are obliged to follow. The world's foremost leaders met in Basel, just as they did in Vienna.

Basel is already part of the past, but no truly effective response has been provided for financial crises, it appears.

The concept of various authorities assigned to safeguarding delicate sectors has only shifted the problems to other areas, without resolving the root causes.

We have seen that the system of authorities which become the guardians of relations between citizens (consumers, investors) and market operators (banks, listed companies) does not always produce positive outcomes, especially in cases where the authorities themselves remain "caught in the net", yielding to the blandishments of those they should be supervising.

Juvenal long ago brought up the question of who guards the guardians, who watches the watchdogs.[243]

Fundamentally, there does not seem to be a solution to the problem of control, of the supervision of supervisors. The fact that there currently exists no solution does not mean that there no solution is possible; it may even mean that there are multiple solutions.

The system can be left exactly as it is today. The States, once they have agreed to follow a common approach, intervene, hopefully in the least possible measure, in cases in which the authorities fail in their job; some corrective measures, such as provision for authorities' liability, could be established. The limit, which has been fully illustrated, of this first solution lies in the subtle art of bypassing the remedy practised by those who should apply it; the defence of discretionary power that is "indisputable" by nature, and the limitation of cases of liability to gross negligence or malice are only two examples.

The second solution consists in strengthening the authorities' activity, giving them instruments of control and, therefore, also strengthening their liability. In addition to the limits of the first solution there exists the danger of hypertrophy in the system, obscuring the principle of the certainty of the law and of the effectiveness of its administration.

The third solution, perhaps the most radical, consists in totally eliminating all hypocrisy linked with instruments which are only apparently decentralised and independent, leaving the market free to follow its course, and thus allowing banks and consumers to regulate themselves.

To return to Juvenal's metaphor, the proposed hypothesis would be that husbands (the States) should trust their wives (citizens and consumers) and avoid calling on guardians to keep at bay those who dangerously threaten the domestic hearth (the banks). This could be the ideal solution, with recourse to legal remedy, the medicine, only in cases of emergency.

Of course it is not easy to understand what the best kind of medicine is.

Still using a health metaphor, Kindleberger's call to study financial crises is still relevant: "at a certain moment, at the beginning of the 19th century, some of the most important medical figures understood that almost all of the complicated treatments then

243 VI Satira Juvenalis: "Pone seram, chibe, sed quis custodiet ipsos custodes? Cauta est et ab illis incipit".

available to treat diseases were not very effective, and various brave doctors [...] suggested that in the majority of cases they did more harm than good. Simultaneously, the surprising discovery was made that some diseases held their own limits, improved on their own, possessed a kind of a 'natural history' [...][244]". Kindleberger identifies the extreme remedy in the figure of the "international lender of last resort", intervening only in cases of international financial crisis. This is an interesting idea which, however, only serves to shift the problem. It is necessary, in fact, to identify who this lender is. And if this lender must be a global player, a new contradiction arises, the circle continues to be vicious. Even Kindleberger, in the almost hopeless attempt to solve the problem, highlights the irremediable contradiction in terms of an international lender of last resort made up of a "club of rich countries (like the Basel club) or an international institution like the IMF (International Monetary Fund)". "I do not see any way of guaranteeing that international rescue operations be free of any suspicion of political favouritism", the author continues.

The international lenders existing when Kindelberger was writing are more or less the same, more than twenty-seven years later: the IMF and the Basel group who continue to "lay the blame upon each other".

Thus the first unsolved issue, if the solution of an *in extremis* intervention is agreed on, concerns the impartiality of the intervening agency.

But there is another issue which needs to be taken into account, which concerns the flexibility of the structure on which the actors depend, the "context which it is possible to enter and exit with the same ease; impossible to imagine a network which does not allow both activities. In a network, connecting and disconnecting are both legitimate choices; they have the same status and they have equal importance".

The network, therefore, appears to have some defects. The first, mentioned above, allows actors to set up "temporary connections" between each other, that may be established and dis-established more easily compared to the traditional model of relations based on a consensus reached by successive agreements. Another, as it were, "endogenous" defect is the extreme rapidity of the spread of disease among those participating in the network. In addition, the "exogenous" defect relates to the difficulty of extending the network towards the peripheries of the world.

The idea propounded by Bauman seems to me to be very close to being utopian. He wishes to find a partial solution, a response to at least the last of the defects listed: "only the global community, an inclusive and not an exclusive community [...] may release the refugees of today's world from the socio-political void in which they have been cast [...]". Furthermore, the same author recognises the utopian nature of a global network that expands to the benefit of the periphery: "As regards the imagined *global* community, such an institutional network (comprising *global* democratic controlling bodies, a legal system which is binding at *global* level and based on ethical principles which are *globally* valid) is largely absent. This, I add, is an important cause, maybe the primary cause, of

244 C.P. Kindleberger, in Euforia e panico, Storia delle crisi finanziarie, Bari, 1981, 140.

what is euphemistically labelled the 'refugee problem', as well as the main obstacle to its resolution".[245]

The difficulty in drawing conclusions lies in not yet having a clear idea on the point. Many elements during the course of writing this thesis have led me to believe that complete homogenisation of models and an increase in their number do not necessarily produce positive effects.

The only sound idea is to continue our search for a way, a direction towards Kantian peace.

The alternative option would be to find time to disconnect from the network, the time necessary to listen to Symphony No. 7 in A major, directed by Beethoven during the Congress of Vienna. A desire for a new season of insurrectionary tumult.

245 K. Bauman, Liquid love: on the Frailty of Human Bonds, Cambridge, 2003, 11.

IUS COMMUNE EUROPAEUM

A peer-reviewed book series in which the common foundations of the legal systems of the Member States of the European Community are the central focus.

The *Ius Commune Europaeum* series includes horizontal comparative legal studies as well as studies on the effect of treaties within the national legal systems. All the classic fields of law are covered. The books are published in various European languages under the auspices of METRO, the Institute for Transnational Legal Research at Maastricht University.

Recently published:
Volume 75: *The Principle of Numerus Clausus in European Property Law*, B. Akkermans
Volume 76: *European Cooperation between Financial Supervisory Authorities, Tax Authorities and Judicial Authorities*, M. Luchtman
Volume 77: *Access to Justice and the Judiciary: Towards New European Standards of Affordability, Quality and Efficiency of Civil Adjudication*, A. Uzelac and C.H. Van Rhee (eds.)
Volume 78: *The European Private Company (SPE): A Critical Analysis of the EU Draft Statute*, D.F.M.M. Zaman, C.A. Schwarz, M.L. Lennarts, H.-J. De Kluiver and A.F.M. Dorresteijn (eds.)
Volume 79: *Constitutions Compared. An Introduction to Comparative Constitutional Law*, 2nd edition, A.W. Heringa and Ph. Kiiver
Volume 80: *Rechtsbescherming en overheidsovereenkomsten. De preventieve en jurisdictionele rechtsbescherming bij de gunning van overheidsovereenkomsten in Nederland, Frankrijk en België en de mogelijke invloed van de rechtspraak van het Hof van Justitie*, K. Wauters
Volume 81: *Derden in het contractenrecht*, I. Samoy (red.)
Volume 82: *The Right to Specific Performance. The Historical Development*, J. Hallebeek and H. Dondorp (eds.)

www.ingramcontent.com/pod-product-compliance
Ingram Content Group UK Ltd.
Pitfield, Milton Keynes, MK11 3LW, UK
UKHW051928100926
8556IPUK00022B/1435